Oy Mame! Oy Mame!

I Looked into the Eyes of Evil

The Life of Holocaust Survivor Abraham Gutreiman

BY

CHANA GUTREIMAN GOLDBERG

MAX GUTREIMAN GOLDBERG

MAURICIO VARGAS ORTEGA

3rd Coast Books, LLC
Montgomery, Texas 77356

3rd Coast Books, LLC
19790 Hwy. 105 W. Ste. 1318
Montgomery, TX 77356

www.3rd CoastBooks.com

ISBNs
Perfect Binding (Print) 978-1-946743-36-7
eBook/Mobi 978-1-946743-37-4
eBook/ePub 978-1-946743-38-1

Project Coordinator - Ian W. Gorman, Associate Publisher
Editor - Ian W. Gorman
English Translation - Ariella Garren
Cover Artist – Ileana Carranza Quesada
Cover Coordinator – Theo Viggers
Text Designer – Theo Viggers

Printed in the United States of America

CONTENTS

ACKNOWLEDGEMENT

Ariella Garren was 13 years old when we first met her and her family at the Synagogue in Costa Rica. After reading the Spanish version of our book, Ariella asked us for permission to translate it into English.

Ariella undertook the challenge with great enthusiasm and worked laboriously on the translation.

Upon reading the translation our editor commented on its excellence and could not believe it had been done by such a young girl.

We are deeply grateful for Ariella's excellent work.

— Chana Gutreiman Goldberg
— Max Gutreiman Goldberg

FORWARDS

MEMORIES OF LOVE AND OF DEATH

— Dr. Elizabeth Odio Benito

When World War II finally ended in Europe, on May 8, 1945, with the fall of Berlin, the allied armies that had advanced through the different European countries, encountered the terrors of the concentration camps, the work camps, and the extermination camps organized by the Nazis and their collaborators. Of these camps, spread throughout Germany, Poland, the Netherlands, France, Ukraine, Austria, Italy, Latvia, Czech Republic, Estonia — without this numeration being exhaustive — emerged a genocide without comparison in the history of the human race.

There were millions of deaths, disappeared persons, tortured persons, men, women, children. Auschwitz, Buchenwald, Dachau, Treblinka, Majdanek, Mauthausen, began to be names of sites associated with tragedy and horror that took down European Jews, without any other justification, for being Jews.

As a formal date of the beginning of the genocide, the Night of the Broken Crystals — November 9, 1938 — is often recognized as the beginning of the deportations and creation of the ghettos. But the persecution, deportations, and the deprivation of rights, which the Jews had as citizens of Germany and Poland suffered, had been taking place for years before then.

When the allied soldiers entered the ruins of the camps at the beginning of 1945, the innocent civil victims of the genocides were accounted in millions. Officially, approximately six million Jews, men, women, and children were indicated, plus two million more of non-Jews, handicapped, homosexuals, gypsies, and other "impure" races.

Also, from these ruins, like ghosts that barely were on their feet, women, men, and children emerged, whom their own destiny permitted them to survive, to be witnesses of the most horrifying barbarity ever seen in the history of humanity. Before the astonished and frightened eyes of those who came to help them stand, these victims assumed the faces and the names of all the deceased, to denounce and build a collective memory of what happened.

But the six million human beings in the European camps of death and extermination were not the only victims of the politics on the "Jewish matter", and its "Final Solution", designed by Heinrich Himmler under the murderous anti-Semitic rhetoric of Adolf Hitler, that traveled throughout Europe, and especially Germany since the 1930s. There were other victims and other histories of pain and death, the product of these years and war. There were also in this apocalyptic madness, stories of love, courage, valor, solidarity, sacrifice.

The family history of Abraham and his brother Jacobo Gutreiman is one of those stories. The story of Frieda Goldberg, wife of Abraham, is also one of these stories. This is the story that herein they tell us, with their own voices, from the bottom of their own memories, in the first person, as survivors of the Holocaust.

It is a story soaked with tears, with questions without answers, in forgotten prayers. It is a recounting of lost lives and lived lives. Abraham's dreams, since he was a boy in his natal small Polish town of Parysow, are nightmares. "Where was G-d that night?" "Where were you during all that time of our agony?"

While millions of European Jews were exterminated without their murderers showing any mercy, other millions fled terrified of the ghettos, jumping from the trains of death, they hid in holes; they suffered grueling cold, survived barely eating or drinking. They ran through the war fields, daily evading death, they helped and held onto each other. And sometimes they found small miracles of solidarity by non-Jewish families. Or defenseless, they died of hunger and cold in hostile scenes, with nobody to bury them.

Abraham and Jacobo Gutreiman were among those that fled without stopping and without knowing where to run. Both looked for their mother, for their family; they wanted to survive. Their brother relationship was weaved stronger with the threads of a tragedy that nobody could or can explain. They never were separated. They are the only survivors of their family, now they rest together in the Jewish Cemetery in Costa Rica, a country where they came one day to live almost by chance, looking for the peace that their Polish homeland never gave them. They had their Kaddish and their names are registered in the book of life, as their children wrote at the end of this story.

But Abraham and Frieda, his wife, fulfilled an essential task, that reached out to their children Max and Chana: they transmitted their memories. And they, at the same time, when writing this story, have transmitted it to their children, who must also transmit it to their children and their children to their children. This is what this moving and unique story is about. Of the memory of those who cannot nor must permit silence and oblivion to cover what happened to them and to millions like them, only for being Jews.

There are people that say that the past must be forgotten to live in a present of peace; that you cannot relive the pain or tragedy of the actions that occurred many years before. And even less, maintain the memory alive of those acts in the generations that came after.

This story, *Oy, Mame!*, is a living testimony that we cannot nor must we forget that hate, violence, discrimination, contempt, humiliation, anti-Semitism created the monster of the Holocaust. That Shoah must remain in the present and live in the memory of humanity, so it is not repeated. That the pain and suffering of Abraham and Jacobo through the years where their prayers were not listened to, is a universal story, it is the story of the genocide of the Jewish people. Of their women and men, that for many centuries have pilgrimed throughout the planet looking for peace. And also, it is a mirror, so Jews and we who are not Jews, and all, see ourselves reflected in the way Abraham, Jacobo, and Frieda fought together for life, for peace, with love and courage, now and forever.

DR. ELIZABETH ODIO BENITO
President of the Inter-American Court of Human Rights
Former Minister of Justice, Vice-President of Costa Rica
and Vice-President of the International Criminal Court.

San José, Costa Rica
August 2014

MR. ABRAHAM GUTREIMAN Z"L

— Rabbi Gershon Miletski

Abraham Gutreiman was a name and figure that I carried with me during the fifteen years of service as Rabbi of the Orthodox Jewish Community of Costa Rica. There is no encounter by coincidence. Nothing in this world occurs by coincidence. Each connection has a reason. The history of Abraham Gutreiman summarizes, with great strength and intensity, the history of our people in general and of the previous generation, whose third part was vilely cut.

I had the opportunity to know him very personally and speak with him on many occasions. He was a habitual visitor of the Synagogue for many years and every time he went, he had something to say. Constantly he spoke with the Creator of the Universe: "Where were you at that moment?" Why did you permit these things to happen to our people?"

He, who had experienced in his own flesh, the most difficult experience of that dark epoch, felt that he had the right to ask and demand answers. Frequently he made these questions in my presence as if my help could work to obtain the desired answers.

Even though it was hard for me to listen to him and direct his doubts, I knew that he was not worthy of a warning for the simple reason that he was the only one in body and soul that had forever deep wounds. I sustained that nobody had the right to criticize him, since nobody was in this place at that unbearable time.

I tried to balance his questions with heroic Jewish stories that decided to not let their heads down before the Nazi bestiality, and not go with a bowed head to the killing.

Additionally, the inseparable Gordian knot between him and his brother, Yankel, is a phenomenon that is seen very few times. This connection between brothers that they reached at a respectable age, marked all of his family and each one of them in a crucial manner. This is a marvelous story by itself.

Who permitted this special relationship and supported them with sacrifice during many years was his wife, Mrs. Frieda (may she enjoy a long life), who with the power of her personality directed for many years the family life, raising their children in Germany, Bolivia and later in Costa Rica, where they established themselves for many decades and until this date. There isn't a way to describe or imagine the family's life without her special and dominant personality.

The deceased Mr. Abraham came to the Synagogue every Saturday, every festive day, and Yahrzeit[1] day of his parents and family members, until one day he decided that while he did not receive a satisfactory answer to his doubts, he would not pass through the doorstep of the Synagogue. He continued praying and putting on the tefillin[2] in his house without missing even once. He assured me of it many times. For him, it was important to clarify it. He also completely complied with the Mitzvah[3] of Tallit Katan[4] and he always showed me his Tzitzit[5]. Nevertheless, he did not appear anymore at the Synagogue. It was a strange sensation as if he was "pressuring" the Creator to give him an answer to his questions.

---

[1] Yahrzeit: Yearly anniversary of demise.
[2] Tefillin: In Spanish filacteria, from the Greek phylakteriam which means protection.
[3] Mitzvah: Precept.
[4] Tallit Katan: A small sacred cloak of daily use.
[5] Tzitzit: The Tallit's tassel.

In this way, during a couple of years, he continued with his "stubbornness" and his "protest" and they did not help me with the petitions and the pleads to return to Shil[6], neither of his children, Max and Chana, nor Mrs. Frieda, his wife. They told me, "Give him time, he will return." And in effect, he did. One day he walked with steps that were a little indecisive, and it seemed that he was with hesitation, towards Shil, and since then, until his last day, he did not miss a Saturday nor a festive day, going to the Synagogue and not only to pray. He was one of the fanatics of Torah's speeches. He always had observations or questions of great interest. He also cared, in every way, of the Israeli endeavors. He was a Zionist and pro-Israel with all his being.

The close relationship between us lasted until his last day. I remember when his brother passed away, Yankel Z"L. He sought my closeness and he asked me a lot. I must say that I also enjoyed these conversations a lot. They were very fructiferous for me.

His pride was that his children, Max and Chany, learned and acquired a superior education and became distinguished professionals, without abandoning for any moment their Jewish identity. Also, they mastered the Yiddish language, which was very dear to him. He always awaited happy the opportunity to speak in this language.

Lastly, I would like to conclude with a story that I believe represents the life of Mr. Abraham Z"L. It is the story of "Jason Ish" a very famous Halachic figure of the previous generation, who lived in the city of Bnei Brak, Israel. In the year 1952, a person came near him and asked, "Where can I find a just person (Tzadik)?" The Jason Ish answered,

---

[6] Shil: Synagogue.

"Go tomorrow to the central Synagogue of the city and look for someone that has a blue number in his arm and is putting on the tefillin. He is the just man that you are looking for. That person experienced in his own flesh the darkest horrors of humanity and he daily continues putting on tefillin, this man is pious."

Mr. Abraham Gutreiman Z"L was in this way. A strong man who maintained himself firm. A man that fought for his life and for the life of his family. He was full of questions as a grenade towards the Creator of the Universe, and with all that, he kept putting on tefillin every day, fully complying in this way with the divine commandment. This is Mr. Abraham, who I had the joy of knowing. May he rest in peace.

Rabbi GERSHON MILETSKI
Former Chief Rabbi of the Jewish Community
of Costa Rica for 15 years

A TESTIMONY OF SURVIVAL

— Merida Morales-O'Donnell

This book is a testimony of survival of the horrors of the greatest tragedy of the history of mankind. A moving and poetic description of the discrimination and persecution suffered by Abraham and his brother Yankel, the only surviving members of a Jewish family from Poland. Reading "Oy Mame! Oy Mame!" you hear the voice of Abraham, telling you the journey of his life and that of his brother, moment by moment - an agony of depravations, humiliations, physical aggression, and killings perpetrated by the Nazis against the Jewish population of Poland. "They first killed our souls, and then our bodies".

It is difficult to find words to describe the horrors and grief experienced by these two human beings, examples of the suffering of millions of Jews persecuted and exterminated during the Holocaust. The book reflects Abraham's desire to keep the story alive and pass it on to future generations, in order to prevent its repetition. Unfortunately, the lessons of history are not always followed. Antisemitism and discrimination are features of today's society, racial cleansing occurs in some parts of the world, intransigence and authoritarianism persist, resulting in restrictions to rights and liberties, persecution, and ultimately, displacement. Today's refugees will join Abraham Gutreiman when he moans:

"...we do not occupy a place
in any space; in any time.
We are travelers towards
an uncertain future".

UNHCR was created to help refugees such as Abraham and Yankel. However, its relevance did not end with the resettlement of victims of the Holocaust. Today many more victims of human intransigence remain in need of UNHCR 's help.

Chana Gutreiman surprises me with this book that she, with her brother Max, put together - a vivid testimony of discrimination and persecution resulting from intolerance on religious and racial grounds. I met Chana at the UNHCR Office in Costa Rica in the 1980s and witnessed her kindness and unwavering commitment towards refugees, most of them from Central America, who came to the Office searching for help. Having read the book, I understand why...

MERIDA MORALES-O'DONNELL
Former Director, Americas Bureau,
United Nations High Commissioner for Refugees
June 2021

INTRODUCTION

We were raised in a home formed by our parents an(
to Bolivia from Europe as survivors of the Holocaust.

Our father insisted, day to day in a continuous manner, on telling us all the details of his life in Poland, before, during, and after the Second World War. He had a privileged memory and he remembered in chronological order all the events; this story became our story.

When our father turned 90 years of age, we asked Mr. Jaime Tishler, that he, with his professional video camera, help us eternalize his story. We were conscious that his health was starting to deteriorate, and we did not want his experiences to disappear without being fixed in the memory of our family. Mr. Tishler fulfilled our request with great professionalism and love.

After the death of our father, at the age of 95 years, we decided to collect the recorded information in the videos with memories of the prolonged and unforgettable moments when our father told us his experiences. Our mother, Frieda Goldberg, helped us to review the details and we were able to collect the information that later became the book that we are presenting.

It is of our interest that this book is read by our children Leo and Marina, Harry and Shely, Eitan and Katherine, Sergio and Hilda, Mauricio and Sally, and Alex and Mijal; but above all that this legacy for their children and their children's children is depicted in writing.

— CHANA AND MAX GUTREIMAN

Chapter I

The Faded Lights of Parysow

I

The daily path of a young boy winds through the streets, past the old synagogue, the market, the smells of your kitchen, oh Mother. These are the everyday places where my brothers and sister shone like stars; stars that would later be extinguished. Like that first light in my hometown, that small shtetl, each day, at the crack of dawn, I remember you, Mother.

> *Memory blurs, one light among many;*
> *the cold light of that morning,*
> *the firelight which warmed me like a coat,*
> *the last light in the eyes of*
> *my closest partner on this journey*
> *my one surviving brother.*

All the faces stopped at that moment; even my own face; deteriorating towards nothingness. That eternal instant, as I was thrown from that train, just one, among all the trains that took our People towards their death.

All the exoduses,
All the exiles,
All the fires.
I am frozen in a mirror of shame, Mother
forever dazed.
What of the Fate that faced
everyone left on that train?
You were also left.
Oh, Mother! Oh, Mother!
I will repeat this cry until my last breath.
Oy, Mame! Oy, Mame![7]

II

Have you ever had the feeling of forgetting something? Suddenly you reach a point and you are sure that something was left behind, something important, something essential. I have known people who check over their house ten times before leaving, to make sure that they have not left anything behind. And despite all this exhausting effort, once they are already on the bus or train, far away, without the ability to return, that terrible sensation that something is not okay, returns to them. It is the feeling that they missed something: did I leave the lights on? Did I close the door?

That terrible feeling has always accompanied me. What treasures did I forget in Parysow? How many things were left behind when I departed? Which doors did I forget to close? How many prayers did I forget to raise to Heaven on that last peaceful night of our People?

---

[7] Yiddish: Oh Mother!

2

OY MAME! OY MAME!

Would You have listened to me then?
Would You have turned Your fierce gaze away from us
and the murderous hand of our enemies?
Where were You, G-d, that night?
Where were You in our time of agony?

I am stranded.
Half of me remains a ghost,
forever left behind in a small Polish village.
Half of me is here looking to You.

Do not think that I do not know the objects:
furniture, lamps,
the windows through which
the daylight is already fading.
But behind these surroundings
there is another sky and other stars.
For me, time is not time, but more space.
Anything that strikes my eyes is a potential key,
A key to a door which remains with me,
along with all its tragedy.
a door that opens to my lost childhood.

The long journey along a steep and stony slope started for me on January 17, 1917. I was born in Parysow in the Siedlecki province, located 10 kilometers from Garwolin and 50 kilometers from Warsaw. I remember it as a small, peaceful place, but back then, shadows never stopped darkening objects or the faces that watched, like they do now. Son of an eternal people, heir to a history of slavery, struggles, exile, and persecution; my blood, from such an early age, had known that tragedy in the humble town of my nostalgia and my nightmares.

The first Jews settled in Parysow around the 18th century. Large Jewish populations also inhabited nearby towns. The *Tzadik*[8] Jehoshua Asher Rabinovitz came from Želechow in the middle of the 19th century, the son of a respected Rabbi from Przysucha. He brought with him an especially important group of Hasidic Jews. His teachings lived on in his children Jacob Tzvi and Meir Shalom. Jehoshua Asher's influence spread to Parysow and beyond. There were several rabbis in Parysow, but the spiritual leader was the Rabbi Shie Use, who was married and had many children.

My parents were born in Parysow, like me. I was the sixth child, after four boys and a girl. My older brother, Moschiche was married at age 20 to Esther Faige Gutman. They had four children: Moshe, Yoshi, Vigde, and one daughter, whose name I have forgotten. My second brother, Velvu, was married at age 24 to our first cousin, Malka. She had once been engaged but the betrothed broke the bond that would unite them. My mother, hurt by this, insisted that it was unacceptable that she should suffer this way, and married my brother to her. They had three children. My sister Roise followed, and she married Zeilig Mlotek. They had two children: Mortje and Rivkale.

Roise's marriage with Zeilig has a story of its own. When my sister reached the age of 14, my mother stopped sleeping at night. She was in a state of extreme anguish; she feared she would not have enough money for a nadn, or dowry, to give to her daughter for her marriage. She thought that at least 3500 zlotys (Polish currency) were necessary as a dowry. Fortunately, with all of us working, our financial situation improved considerably, so we worked together and collected the money, which she kept in a small drawer in her nightstand. One day, the rabbi of Parysow told my mother he wished to marry his son to our sister Roise. My mother could not have been more pleased with the idea. She considered it the greatest honor my sister and our family could possibly receive. That young man was surely the most dignified

---

[8] In Judaism a title given to a righteous person.

suitor that Roise could hope for in the whole village. But we, the children, knew the misery of cold and starvation. We understood that we had to work hard in order to escape that harsh fate and to move forward. We weren't as enthusiastic as our mother was, so we let her know.

"How can our sister marry a scholar?" we said. "From what will they live? Think of what will happen. He will be studying the Torah all day; they cannot live on that. Knowledge does not fill the stomach."

Although my mother considered that marriage a great honor, there were more of us. And we insisted that Roise needed a young, brave working man with ambition; a responsible entrepreneur who could ensure our sister a stable, relaxed life, without the anguish that hunger and misery brought. It was then that Zeilig Mlotek came along. He was a 20-year-old farmworker. Mlotek united with us as part of the family, always ready to help. He traded with barley and became an accomplished man.

Yankel (Jacob) followed Roise, and he married Golde. (Before marriage, her name was Chana. She shared my mother's name, so it was necessary that she change it, because Ashkenazi Jewish tradition forbids two living members of the same family to share a name. Unlike Sephardi Jews, we honor our dead by naming new family members after them. Golde was the daughter of a rabbi and attended the Beit Yaacov school for religious girls. She worked as a teacher and gave my mother two grandchildren: Sara Peiru and Chaim Mortje.

Pinche, whose name comes from the biblical figure Pinchas, was the youngest of the older brothers. Later, while we were living in the ghetto, Pinche went to study Torah in the house of two brothers, who lived in a shtibu[9], the study house, of the Gerer rabbi. They had

---

[9] Also referred to a Shtiebel or Shtibl.

one sister and they watched over her as their parents had been murdered by the Nazis. A neighbor saw my brother entering and leaving their house. The gossip began. It was said that Pinche did not go there to study the Torah but to see the girl. When my mother learned of the gossip, gaining more and more strength, she insisted that Pinche marry the girl named Dama since her condition as an orphan made her especially vulnerable to what people might say. My brother, of course, did so.

I was not the youngest of our family. I always knew that I had a younger brother who died as an infant.

My father was named Mortje Izrok. He was, without doubt, an entrepreneur, like many of the men and women of our people have been throughout the generations. He was a man used to facing the challenges of life; a fighter; committed to G-d, with his faith and his family.

My family was quite religious. Our lives revolved around the synagogue. I can remember it to this day. As if time never drew us apart, and daily prayers would soon be beginning just like they used to.

> *I imagine the faces and the eternal light.*
> *I feel the cold, damp smell of the stones,*
> *a familiar warmth returns to embrace me,*
> *to warm my tired bones.*
> *Through the furniture and the walls of Your holy room —*
> *through Your eyes — I see the Temple Mount.*
> *Through my shoes, I feel the cold grey floor*
> *that supports the weight of our faith and our heavy doubts.*

Our Synagogue, that beautiful, holy place, built in the late 19th century, never lacked a *minyan*,[10] never had the Torah stopped to

---

[10] A quorum of a minimum ten men, all over the age of 13, required for certain religious obligations.

be read, *Tefillah*[11] not said, and the *Kaddish*[12] not recited. The blessing of the *Cohanim*[13] was never lacking in a Jewish population, faithful to the G-d of our ancestors. As the synagogue was Orthodox, men and women prayed separately; men on the ground floor and women on the second floor. The Torah was studied in the *Beis Medrash*[14] and prayers were held even at night, without excluding the children. In the Sacred Ark of the synagogue, *the Torah Scrolls*[15] were kept like treasures.

During the Jewish year, the Torah is read on Mondays, Thursdays, Saturdays, and holidays. The entire reading of the Torah finishes on Simchat Torah. In my village, celebrations were held in the humble cobbled streets of Parysow, dancing jubilantly with the Torah scrolls. Although Simchat Torah is celebrated in all the synagogues of the world, it is not in every village that you find dances through the streets with the holy scrolls.

We lived our Judaism naturally, as an inherent part of our lives. We were respectful of tradition. On Fridays, the gabbai[16] would announce the arrival of Shabbat and all the families attended synagogue. On Purim, families would exchange visits and gifts. On Rosh Hashanah we would head to the synagogue full of faith, to thank G-d for the year that passed and beg compassion and blessings for the one that would start.

There was also a Jewish cemetery where our bones would rest. It was our destiny as Jews, as human beings rooted in a land, to our eternal faith. But we do not participate in the writing of the Book of Life. If anything, we suggest, tentatively, a comma, a period, an adjective, a verb, a small change that does not usually fit with the

---

[11] Jewish prayers.

[12] Jewish prayer for the soul of the deceased.

[13] Descendants of Biblical Aaron that became the Jewish priestly class.

[14] Jewish study hall located in the synagogue.

[15] The holiest books of Judaism made up of the five books of Moses.

[16] A person who assists in the running of synagogue services.

dynamics of the Universe. From a very young age, we were taught to pray in Hebrew and to read Yiddish in the *cheder*.[17] To learn Polish I had to attend the local public school. This was not normal for a Jewish boy at the time, so I had to convince my family, especially my mother, to allow it.

Sometimes I wonder,
with grief,
if it really made sense for me
to ever learn Yiddish.
They killed so many of our people.
So many years have passed.
and there is no one left
to write to
in our native tongue
our Mama Loshen.

And so, I started attending public school. I went without a yarmulke on my head. Some members of the community reproached me. But I would not change my mind. I studied until age ten, reading and writing in Polish, and they even taught me to pray Mass. I recall it to this day. At age ten I stopped attending school.

Nostalgia, to most, means the memory
of happy times that have passed.
Times of prosperity, of balance and stability
A shining spring afternoon with happy faces,
the soft smell of fresh fruit,
the sweet taste of happiness.

---

[17] Elementary Jewish school in which children are taught the Torah and other books in Hebrew.

8

OY MAME! OY MAME!

I cannot count myself among those lucky ones.
My memory was born of tragedy.
On the day my father was murdered
my baby brother would also die.

I remember that day at school when my mother came to look for me, so I would go to work. That was my reality, and I never complained. Thanks to the fact that I learned to work at a young age, I would one day be able to bring my family forward, achieving the miracle that I would never lack anything truly essential in my home.

But it was not easy for a little boy of ten to find work. Often, I had to beg. I tried to explain the necessities of my family, my situation as an orphan, and my obligation to help my mother with the hard work of ensuring our livelihood. Finally, someone trusted me.

He explained to me: "I buy wheat seeds here and then travel 50 kilometers to Warsaw, where I resell them in the market. I often buy 200 kilos, and I rent a cart with horses to be able to bring them. I will give you 10 kilos, and you will try to sell them. You can be by my side."

Grateful for the opportunity, I accepted. We traveled six hours on an awful road. When we reached Warsaw, I placed my merchandise next to my benefactor's and started offering my product. After a while, a client arrived and bought all my 10 kilos of wheat. I would have wanted to keep selling, but that was all the help the man would give.

I managed to earn my first 5 zlotys with that trade. I was proud, but also hungry. I remember how I yearned to eat a piece of bread, a sour pickle, and a goose meat jerky. I started to calculate the costs:

If I buy the bread, the pickle, and the goose jerky,
I will spend 1.50 zloty.
For the transport home, I will need another 1.50 zloty,
which will amount to 3 zlotys.
If I pay these costs,

I will only have 2 zlotys to offer to my mother.
So, I reach a wise decision:
I will not eat anything.
And the 50 kilometers to home,
I will walk.

Excitedly, I told my older brother about my experience selling grains in the Warsaw market. He was enthusiastic about the idea and proposed that we try our luck establishing a stall at the market to sell grain at the capital; taking care, of course, not to invade the space of the good man who had taken pity on my needy situation. It started to go well for us. As soon as we could, my mother went to pay the good man back the 5 zlotys that he let me earn with his grains.

My mother was a proud woman in a good way. She would not let others view her with pity. "That is why we have our hands," she would say, "so we can work and be a united front against all odds."

Though we were very young, we worked like men, taking responsibility for one another. All the money we earned would go to our mother, who managed it. If someone needed anything, they would ask our mother for money. It was a good system for everyone, but most of all for my mother, so she could look out for us.

It was in that time of emerging well-being, that my oldest brother, just 21 years old, was drafted into the army. Desperate, my mother wrote to the military man in charge of recruitments. Her argument was that, as a widow, her eldest son was in charge of providing a livelihood for the members of the family. My mother expressed that if my brother joined the war effort, we would die of hunger, and furthermore, she was a sickly woman who suffered from constant fainting and often had to take *kogot*[18] pills for her headaches.

---

[18] Analgesic pills.

After two or three of my siblings were married, the matchmaker approached my mother with a *shidduch*[19] for her; Mother did not accept. She was very dedicated to us and to religion. My mother prayed at the door of the synagogue and was the batville[20] who guided the women during prayer.

As though it were a dark omen, it was the cemetery of Parysow, of all the places of my village, that provoked my greatest sadness. It was a tragic place for me. It makes sense, one might say, to feel this of a cemetery. But, in my case, the feeling was deeper, more internal. No one knows the date it was built. It is known, however, that it was before the Tzadik Rabinovitz died in 1862. It was located in the forest, close to a railroad crossing. Nearly all of it was destroyed during the war. Only one gravestone is left today. The tomb of the Tzadik has ceased to exist. I found a letter that the current residents of Parysow sent to the Jewish Historical Institute. It read, "At present, there are indications of a Jewish presence in Parysow. The cemetery survived for many years but was gradually demolished. The gravestones were used to rebuild the burnt village. The area of the old cemetery is now covered by pine trees."

Some Polish gentiles desecrated the Jewish tombs, motivated by the tale that we were buried with treasure. With which treasures could we have been buried? We had only our faith, our love, and our pain, and those of our ancestors; our only treasure a dignified death by natural causes and not by baseless violence and the hate of relentless enemies.

Even those who later escaped the extermination camps were not permitted to rest peacefully. They, too, were violated and their remains torn from the sacred ground. Recovering the bones scattered here and there would be as impossible as gathering sand, a macabre puzzle.

---

[19] Shidduch, a match.
[20] Or Ba'al Tefillah, the woman who lead the women's prayers.

11

In the autumn of 2006, a representative of the Warsaw Jewish community dedicated himself to cleaning the graves. He presented an official complaint before the municipal office that the site of the old cemetery, now covered with trees, part of the forest, an isolated, limitless place, would be cleared. It is reached by a public road and there are no fences or doors that prevent desecration. I do not know if the Municipality took that complaint into consideration.

Today there are no gravestones.
Like so many others
the cemetery fell victim to racial hatred.
No common graves are recognized.
No structures remain.
Nothing calls the attention of a passerby.
And the overgrown vegetation
plays obstacle to reaching this forgotten place,
a silent monument
to the nameless violence
suffered by our people.

My father also knew violence, greed, and hatred. He also succumbed to the injustice of the world. His remains cannot rest as they deserve in a sacred place.

My father had put all of his hope into the thought of buying a house. He knew that owning a place means prosperity for the whole family. Like harvesting on fertile land, not throwing seeds to the sea; building on rock and not sand; stability. Near Parysow, around 10 kilometers away, is the town of Garwolin. In this town, my father already managed to place a deposit for what might have been our house. He was happy. It was the culmination of great sacrifice. How much must my parents have worked to save what was necessary and buy that house? How many deprivations? How many long journeys of incessant work, to be able to reach that bountiful dream?

OY MAME! OY MAME!

It is said that
if you want to make G-d laugh,
you tell him your plans!

My father was so full of happiness that he was not cautious. His pure soul could not harbor evil. Perhaps only a person who lives and grows surrounded by evil has the means to defend against it. This happened to my father and, as I would later understand, to our people too.

My father could not see the shadow
threatening to cover us,
and our people could not react in time
to defend from the evil that would cover us all.
So Evil has the advantage.
It hides,
stealthily planning its attack,
studying its victim,
and waiting for the opportune moment
to strike the fatal blow.

My father told everyone the details of the negotiation. Many knew the amount of the purchase, the down payment that had been given, his meetings with a lawyer, and the place and time at which the deal would be closed. This was dangerous information to share. But he had not the capacity to suspect the evil, the envy, the hatred hidden in the human soul. We would soon have the opportunity to see it emerge, shameless and brazen, the Polish hatred of the Jew.

Sometimes it takes no more than an instant
for your life to change forever.
Who can wake up one morning
and know how the day will end?
Tell me sincerely;

13

are we not subject to chance?
Do we not know that those simplest circumstances
could influence our destiny?
How might we tell
if this light coming through the window
and illuminating our faces
will be the last
for you and me?

One fateful day, and my life and the lives of my family changed forever. My father had asked a young Polish man to accompany him to Garwolin to finalize the buying of our house. Father was thirty-two years old, and the young man was an acquaintance of his. Bringing him along for such an important matter, perhaps my father considered him a friend. Four kilometers from Garwolin, that young "friend" murdered my father.

The man who had accompanied him murdered him, to steal the money with which he was about to buy the house that we would only dream of living in. Due to the circumstances of his death, on land belonging to Garwolin village, the body was transferred there to perform an autopsy. Autopsy is forbidden, a desecration, according to Jewish Law.

Can you fathom how difficult it is
for me to accept the plans of G-d?
Why did my father, a religious, responsible,
hardworking, pure-hearted man
suffer this destiny?
Why would G-d let something like this happen?

For wishing for a better life for his family, the payment my father received was betrayal, murder, thievery, desecration after death, a burial without dignity, in the same place where suicides are buried; next to the wall, beyond the Garwolin cemetery.

My mother, Chana Jidis, became a widow at age 30. I remember her telling me that my younger brother died the same day that my father was murdered. She firmly believed that my father took him to relieve my mother of the heavy burden of providing for so many children.

We spent eight days sitting indoors, fulfilling the *shiva*[21]. For eleven months we said Kaddish twice a day, to raise my father's soul on the path towards G-d, and to help ourselves accept his divine will. From then on, my mother's life would be an endless fight to bring us forward.

My father had a tanning floor in partnership with three men: Duved, Yosel, and Mayer. After my father's death, my mother received a letter from the partners in which they told her that she was excluded from the company and could have no benefit from the business. This they said to a woman alone, recently widowed with six mouths to feed. And so from a young age, I understood that economic stability cannot depend on partnerships.

But there was no time to sit and cry. Mama worked hard, with no time to rest. She went out each night, challenging the bitter Polish winter, to deliver food products that she bought and then distributed to restaurants in the provinces.

The death of my father was the first blow that Life hit me with. I have never been able to recover from this loss, or from any of the others.

They are ghosts, you see. Ghosts,
many gaps,
many loopholes, and lots of blood
on lots of hands.

---

[21]The seven-day Jewish mourning period observed by the immediate family of the deceased.

It cannot be washed off even with
a lifetime of washing.

The children in my village would go with their fathers to study the Torah, a fundamental stage of our faith. Each would sit in his father's lap. And if he repeated the Hebrew alphabet correctly, his father would throw him a sweet. The children were told that those sweets came from the angels up in heaven, rewarding them for their effort.

I did not have a lap to sit in, nor sweets from heaven to receive. The angels were not benevolent with me. For me, there was no heaven spilling blessings over my head. What did exist was punishment: beatings if we did not learn. My reality was an absence, a great emptiness that my father left behind.

This is why, my child, I have given you your name and I will always call you *Tate*[22]. Somehow you relieved this pain. You have given me the opportunity of declaring a word so big and so great, capable of warming the winter, lighting the night, and purifying the silence.

---

[22] In Yiddish Father.

Chapter II

Wolves and Warnings

I

How silent is death!
It arrives like the cold
that starts seeping through your feet,
inching its way towards freezing your soul.
Like wolves at night, death lashes out.
His harbingers arrive with callous hands;
steely eyes intimidating the dawn.
One must stay in the shadows,
feeling their presence as they burst through the door,
panting with luminous eyes.
One watches them from an invisible place,
feeling the fear that has materialized
and runs an unthinkable cold down the back.
The wolves smell terror, coursing through the veins.
They grin horribly, illuminating the night.
So one can only wait, knowing that the clumsy and imprecise
route of survival is part of a dreadful game.
Knowing that wolves sense death surrounding us,
carrying it in their bloodstained jaws.

II

In 1933, Germany was going through a difficult stage and the environment was dismal. Millions of unemployed people roamed the grey streets like specters, and despair left its impression on society. The worldwide crisis threw a blow at a country, whose generations could still remember times of greatness and hope to heal its wounds. Fifteen years earlier, German pride had been dragged through the mud. The outcome of the First World War had left a long-term lack of confidence in the Germans and in their feeble government. And how dangerous that feeling can be, especially in a whole nation. That situation was the precipitating factor for the emergence of a leader, Adolf Hitler, Supreme Leader of the German National Socialist Workers Party.

Hitler was a great speaker and a snake charmer who introduced a dreary, anxious Germany to an instant, extreme solution. The Hitlerian discourse came out strongly among Germans of all social classes. He promised them a better life, a vigorous new Germany that would earn back its former splendor in a matter of years. He promised a Germany that would be the light of Europe, shining above the powers that had humiliated them during World War I.

Hate was the mortar of those speeches, and vengeance and destruction the bricks. The homeland, like an ancient barbaric deity, demanded a holocaust, a suitable victim to quench its thirst for fire and blood. Hitler stepped forth to offer the sacrifice, knowing that the masses would yell with rage and enthusiasm at the bloody ceremony. Hitler's ascent to power and the consumption of his apocalyptic speeches were quick and definitive. In 1939, Hitler's military forces invaded Poland with the intention of annexing it to Nazi Germany. "Operation Fall Weiss" began on September 1st, and on October 6th the surrender of the Polish army was consolidated. Poland was the first victim of the expansionist ambition of Germany. With all the fury of their famous *blitzkrieg,*[23] the Polish army was easily defeated. The German occupation violently changed the lives of the Polish, and our lives, the lives of Polish Jews.

Again, our people became the target of hate and persecution. The European powers showed a casual indifference to this tragedy. France and the United Kingdom did not raise their voices to denounce the German massacre.

They would not see past Hitler's false promise, that he had no interest in starting a conflict. They would pay dearly for their indifference, but not as dearly as we did. This reality marked the beginning of the Second World War.

The wolf pack is born
of German desperation, hunger, and poverty.
The beasts must be fed
with the historical hatred and resentment
championed by the major genocide.
Then the wolves,
thirsty for blood and power,
come out of their cave
and are now racing across Europe.
The time of
Horror, Persecution, and Death
has arrived.

Parysow was occupied by the German Army in September of 1939, during the invasion. It was just before Rosh Hashana. From the beginning, we knew that the night, collapsing on our heads, would never again return to day.

---

[23] "Lightning War", method of attack used by the German army consisting of surprise and ferocious bombings and rapid troop advancement.

The first thing they demanded was that we deliver the warm clothes with which we would protect ourselves from the harsh winter. They knew that at the first gust of cold, the weakest would not survive. The penalty for getting caught wearing warm clothes, in an attempt to withstand the frost, was death. Even from the start, they showed cruelty without borders.

Many Polish non-Jews collaborated with the Germans. They became the informers who, for one kilogram of sugar, would deliver entire families to the murderous ferocity of the invaders. The Germans did not call us by our names. I imagine they were trying to dehumanize us, to make us seem more like animals than human beings; a plague that had to be exterminated; moreover, it was a patriotic duty to undertake. To call us by our names would be to admit that we were humans like them; that like them, we deserved the right to live and work and fall in love and have children and dream and die old and happy, having truly lived life.

They forced us to pay 100 zlotys for each family member, every so often, and they placed a yellow *Magen David*[24] on our arms, to be able to identify us as Jews. The businesses that many had built from the ground up, due to many years of hard work, were looted by the Nazis. They would enter whenever they felt like it, smash the glass, throw out our hard-earned products to the street, and beat down owner and employee alike. They did not take it all away, but they made sure that the first thing they took was our dignity and our rightful pride as human beings.

When they took our clothing and our businesses, and then our homes, we were no more than shadows of what we had once been. This is the part of the story, which I think, many do not understand. The Germans first wounded what was most sacred to us: our respect, our confidence, and our sense of security. Our life-long neighbors fueled by fear, hunger, and/or hatred informed on us to the authorities. They

---

[24] Star of David.

killed some important part of us, before finishing our lives. It was the perfect plan, Evil for Evil's sake. They first killed our souls and then our bodies.

And what cunning it took to sow betrayal and treachery even within our own people. They called it the Judenrat, a council made up of Jews and established by the mandate of the Germans. In every Jewish population of Europe occupied by the German army, the Judenrat had to exist.

The Germans demanded its existence, so they could execute Nazi interests within the Jewish community. Obviously, any self-respecting Jew did not want to be part of the force that would almost always become a betrayal. The Germans would request, for a certain date, a specific number of Jews. The organization had about ten Polish policemen who were the ones in charge of fulfilling the orders of arresting and delivering the necessary Jews. Many times, they used them for forced labor or in the service of some German military man of greater rank, but the final destiny of the great majority was death. The subtlety of the German scheme was masterful, its main objective clear: to degrade the Jews before their total extermination. More than vile, the Jews who were part of the Judenrat were humiliated; forced to give the order to deliver their people to the butchers. And, in the end, they would also take their places in the Nazi slaughterhouse.

Beneath the surface, the Judenrat were simply Jews trying to protect their own as best they could, obtaining privileges like food, or clothing. They were made to believe they could count on their friendship with the Germans; that they were safe from the rigor and violence with which they treated others.

The village *shochet*[25] had a son who not only became part of the Judenrat but became its president. The son of the shochet led himself

---

[25] A person certified to slaughter cattle and poultry in the manner prescribed by Jewish law.

to believe he was a friend of the Germans. That feeling of security gave him the confidence to wield his authority over the Polish policemen.

He thwarted their desire to do whatever they wanted, and they resented being held back by the growing authority of the privileged Jew. And so, the Polish Police decided to take revenge on the president of the Judenrat, who had lost all perspective of the danger threatening any Jew in that situation.

The Police killed a goose and took it to the house of the shochet, father of their supposed boss. Goose in hand, they went to the Germans, showing them that this man was killing the animals according to the sworn ritual, a forbidden action, punishable by death. The Germans imprisoned not only the father but also their "close friend" the president of the Judenrat.

Desperate, wanting to save his life, the wife of the soon-to-be-dead man, incriminated three other Jews from Stock, a town near Zelechow. One might say that these five were killed that night for no crime but a false accusation. But the truth is that they were murdered for being Jewish; nothing more.

Bit by bit, what were once our lives were left in ruins. In 1944 the Nazis destroyed the synagogue. Its stones were the flesh and soul of our people.

How nice it is that the stone,
when torn from its foundations,
recognizes the way back to its former splendor
and becomes a stone again.

Even flesh in some way
also returns and is reborn.
Only the soul, once destroyed,
can never return from eternal silence.

OY MAME! OY MAME!

It will wander the corridors of memory
without arms or legs,
and with one eye will watch the same portrait
of its misery for eternity.

Chapter III

Surrounded by Shadows

I

I am isolated.
With the passage of time
my jail extends past
the roughness of its former walls,
the nauseating smell of the caverns,
the invisible borders of the ghetto.

Now I am stranded
in my memories, in my dreams,
forever bound by darkness;
in Guilt that is heavier than chains.

I am isolated.
I do not know if it is the same place,
but a different time.
I do not know if time has stopped,
become a fire, searing my soul.

We were shadows
fading in a sinister evening.
No wall could contain us,
because the shadow is proof
that things occupy a place
in the intricate sieve of the universe.

But we do not occupy a place
in any space; in any time.
We are travelers towards
an uncertain future.

This morning also,
I have awakened
in the circle of shadows.

II

I n 1942, we were permanently taken from our homes. The ghetto of Parysow was established. The growing divide between Jews and Polish gentiles was clearer than ever. The order given was clear, inflexible, and ruthless:

"Leaving the ghetto means death."

Those who died for disrespecting the order were not few, my brother Pinche among them. It is not easy to die of hunger, slowly, gradually, and it is even harder to see loved ones eaten away, to be forced to watch in helplessness. Is it better to die feebly or to sacrifice your life fighting for it? Food was scarce in the ghetto and yet the population grew every day. In our community, there were around 500 people, but Jews from elsewhere arrived, and the ghetto population amounted to around 8,000. Some escaped from their villages hoping to find a place to elude the death that threatened them, but they only ended up dying in a strange land.

It was crowded. The hygienic conditions, the lack of food, and the desperation were too much for most. A typhus plague claimed many lives. We tried to collect our dead from the streets, to take them to the synagogue, and bury them in pits that we dug. We preferred that than to allow the Germans to take the bodies without any respect or mercy.

The Polish government, a puppet of the invading forces, had passed a law banning *kosher* meat. Jews could be killed whichever way the Nazis fancied, but cows and chickens could not be sacrificed according to the ancient Jewish law of *kashrut*. This is a cruel display of the hypocrisy and double standards that history must charge the Poles, who offered their Jewish compatriots as sacrifices to save their own skin. Nine of every ten Jews living in the Parysow ghetto were poor and in great need; even more so after the ban of *kosher* sacrifice.

Fortunately, some non-Jewish butchers wanted to help us and devised a plan: Jewish butchers sacrificed the animals according to the law of kashrut, then veterinaries shot the animals so it seemed that they had died by the bullet and not according to the Jewish ritual. The plan was successful and *kosher* meat was sent from the ghetto to Warsaw.

Those were days of scarcity, of hunger without hope. I remember, once, a woman risked leaving with her daughter to look for food outside the ghetto. The Germans caught them and murdered them on the spot. The father (and grandfather) of the mother and daughter went to the Judenrat, begging it to allow the bodies to be buried in the Jewish cemetery.

The Judenrat, frightened, said, "If you go for the bodies and the Nazis find out, they will come and kill 100 of us in retaliation for having disobeyed their orders. Is it worth sacrificing 100 alive for two dead?"

But the man insisted and implored the Judenrat, "If the Germans find out, I will hand myself over to them to kill me. But I have no choice but to go get them so they can be buried according to our customs."

So great was the insistence of the man, so many his tears and so deep and sincere his pain, that the heart of the Judenrat softened and they allowed the man to go out to look for his daughter and granddaughter. Fortunately, the Germans did not discover him, and he fulfilled his obligation, as mandated by the Jewish law and his wounded heart.

My older brother, Moshiche, also risked leaving the ghetto accompanied by one of his sons, a boy of thirteen. They went to the market to buy food from the Poles, but the Germans caught sight of them and began to pursue them. My brother managed to escape, but the Germans captured my nephew.

With harsh words and threats he was interrogated, "Who is this man you were with?"

The boy replied, as his father had told him to, "I don't know him. I met him on the way and we simply walked together."

The Germans brought my nephew before the Judenrat. Taking advantage of the fact that there was a shift change in the German soldiers, my nephew begged the men of the Judenrat, "Please, bring a corpse in my place and let me go. Do not let the Germans kill me."

The Judenrat did not dare, too afraid of being caught by the Germans to save a life. What they did was advise my nephew, "When the Germans return and they see you here, they will interrogate you and ask you what you have done and why you have been brought here. So, you will tell them you do not know why they brought you here, that you were walking at the borders of the ghetto when the soldiers captured you and took you here."

When the Germans returned, my nephew followed the advice given by the Judenrat. The soldiers let him go, but not before beating him and spitting on him.

My brother Pinche did not have such luck. By then, he was married and expecting his first child. Concerned about the health of his family, my brother left the ghetto to get food, which grew increasingly scarce. He did it a first time and was able to return safely. The success of his first trip motivated him to venture out a second time, but some Polish gentiles saw him in the market and immediately went to the Germans and told them, "This here is a Jew, and this is not the first time he left the ghetto."

That is how the Germans arrested Pinche and brought him before the Judenrat, who tried without success to have him forgiven. My sister-in-law, very advanced in her pregnancy, knelt, desperate, kissing their feet, crying, and begging them to forgive her husband, not to leave her son orphaned before he was even born. Her cries were worth nothing.

The heart of the wolves is cold.
The tremble of the victim,
far from sparking mercy in their souls,
incites the attack,
inflaming the blood in their veins
as their muzzles show the salivation
produced by the desire to kill,
to drink the blood of their victims.

The Nazis put Pinche in a cart. They allowed his wife, my mother, and me to accompany him. They took us out of the ghetto and to a wooded area. We were all distressed and afraid, our souls tormented by a terrible pain.

The journey lasted for centuries, and when my brother realized that we approached the place of his death, he turned to his wife and said, "I will never see our child born." Then he turned to our mother and spoke, "Mother, now you will have one less son."

That memory still torments my nights. Those would be the last words of my brother, who was torn from us and taken to the forest, from where he would never return.

My nephew, the orphaned son of Pinche, would be born
dead a few days later.

Chapter IV

Never Ending Trains

I

The trains keep going.
They run through a night as long as Your absence.
I hear them arrive with their metallic groans.
Their dark wagons, with the faces of horror
peering out from within.

The trains always go to the same place.
Never did a train know another destination.

I always want to go out,
run to the nearest platform,
wait with others for the arrival;
approach with others
the worn-out machines
that time paints a nostalgic green.

But I never get there.
When I hear the metallic whistling
made of screams,
the train is already far away.

35

It speeds through the night so quickly
that I could not jump
to my escape this time.
I would have to go with the train to a distant death.

I would arrive at the platform one morning.
The sun would shine.
The war would have gone
with the winter
and we would all
embrace each other again,
celebrating the awakening
from the menacing nightmare
of the sinister trains.

II

On September 27, 1942, the Germans came for us. Their orders were to transfer all Jews from Parysow to Treblinka. No words can describe the horror, the anguish that gripped us at that moment. Despite all the tragedies, of the grief that we did not even have time to absorb, of the atmosphere of death that had descended over our heads since the arrival of the Germans, we wanted to live. We could not resign ourselves to the imminent death that we knew awaited us at Treblinka. Hundreds of Jews tried to save themselves by fleeing through the woods.

The Germans, who knew about this, went through the list in the ghetto to know exactly how many of us had escaped. At the end of the recount, a young soldier announced:

"We are missing 1,000 heads."

That was what they called us — *"heads"* — as if we were animals; a plague of lowly creatures that must be eliminated for the public good, for the sake of the "pure race" that Hitler had exalted in his speeches.

What followed was one of the darkest episodes of all. Although we had always felt a separation between Jews and Gentiles, we never thought that in those eyes that watched us, sometimes with suspicion, so much hatred was hidden. Were they not our neighbors, our companions?

We Jews had arrived in Poland 1,000 years before; did that not give us the right to feel as Polish as our gentile neighbors?

I have often wondered what happened to those souls. We were exterminated, and entire families disappeared. Of my family, only Yankel and I survived. In very few families did two members survive, when the average number of children was six or seven. They ended our lives, in one way or another. Those of us who have remained alive have only suffered, unsuccessfully searching for fragments of who we once were.

But what about them? The Poles who sold their lifelong neighbors? Those who witnessed the parade of the same faces they had always seen in the market, in the square, on the river, in the then ghostly streets of Parysow. What became of them, of those souls? How could they continue to live with the remorse, the guilt? Poland was a cursed country then. Many years, perhaps centuries will have to pass to erase the blood on those hands; blood inherited by their children and their children's children.

On the loudspeakers the Germans announced:

"HE WHO DELIVERS A JEW WILL BE GIVEN
ONE KILOGRAM OF SUGAR!"

And with that, the hunt began. I remember it as an unspeakable nightmare. It does not matter how many words you use to describe it. I could not, even if I had all the words in the world. The Jews shrieked. The Poles chased us like dogs, their eyes bloodshot, red with hatred and greed. The Poles beat us; they dragged us. Some tried to catch three, four, or five Jews; they knew well that this hunt would mean a kilogram of sugar per head.

The Germans arrived to announce that the next day we would be transferred. We managed to escape to Jeshin through the back door of the ghetto house. Not all my family could escape. My brother Yankel, who had come to know our state, could not return to his home, where his family was. My sister-in-law Golde, my brother's wife, was dragged to Treblinka along with their children; Sure Peiru, her two-year-old girl, and Chaim Moshe, two months old. In Jeshin, we met again with the family. Among them were my mother and my siblings Moshiche, Velvu, and Roise with their families.

Jews from different villages gathered in the center for displaced people in Jeshin. There they made us sleep on boards, one on top of the other. The overcrowding was frightening. I remember when I arrived. I started looking for a board to sleep on, but after some thought, I made the decision to sleep on the floor since the boards were full of lice.

It was a terrible mistake. At night, the people who slept on the boards removed all the lice they could and threw them on the floor, where I received them. It was horrible. I could not sleep at night.

There are so many lice.
I am useless against them.
I take them off and they come back,
like sorrows, like memories, like Guilt.

To make things worse, I had no other clothing, only an old, ripped shirt and some trousers with holes that I would wear for two years.

When it was time for the distribution of food, we formed endless lines to receive just a little water that they called soup. Then they took us out to force us to do absurd jobs, with the sole intention of humiliating us, laughing at our misery. They told us, for example:

"Jews! Walk twenty steps and dig a hole."

And with that pointless work, they denigrated us. I remember their laughter and our helplessness, our contained anger, and our fear.

Once, we managed to catch a goose and cook it. Yankel advised me, "Remove the skin and with it we will make a soup." So, I did. We sold the meat, and we earned some money.

Some among us had economic resources. I remember a case of a rich man who came to the center to stay. He beckoned to a young man to go to his house and bring him the money. He promised to split it equally. The boy, indeed, went to this man's house but kept all the money to himself. It is impressive how the human being becomes the victim of greed and evil, even in the most difficult and extreme moments.

But we were not safe anywhere. The Germans came to Jeshin, too. They arrived like a pack, shouting, beating, sowing fear and confusion. They wanted to take everyone to Treblinka. That was their mission; that was the order they had received. Exterminate all the Jews, erase them from the face of that cursed land.

Before starting the caravan, the Germans chose a group of Jews at random, to quench their insatiable thirst for blood. They were slaughtered and buried in a common grave. Among them was my brother, Moshiche.

And I remember thinking:
How lucky Moshiche is!
He will not be alone in death.

On the 7th of November, we were transferred to Kalisz, 30 kilometers away. By then we knew that their intention was to send us to Treblinka. Some 3,000 Jews from Stostk led this apocalyptic ceremony. We went on foot as the Germans shouted and shot at the terrified human beings, who saw their own kind fall next to them, perhaps their friends, acquaintances, even brothers, sisters, children, parents. A truck came at the rear. The Nazis picked up the bodies and threw them in without any respect. A few Polish gentiles went with us and were in charge of torturing us, humiliating us; they beat us and demanded that we give them money. What money could we have? We had only hunger left; we had been stripped of everything. I remember that in desperation, we asked G-d:

Why are we here, G-d?
Where are you?
Why are you letting this happen to us?

But we received no answer, only desolation, despair.

The Polish gentiles hurried to remove the belongings of the Jews who were killed by the bullets. The women among us cried desperately; they wanted to get on the truck to accompany their loved ones for the last time, but the Nazis would not let them.

We finally reached a place where there was a wall and, leaning on it, a staircase. The Germans forced us to climb the stairs, to check that there was only an empty space behind the wall. They laughed to see us fall from that height. We waited there until finally, the train arrived that would take us to Treblinka. All the members of my family who still survived got on that train. Our mother met us just before they forced us in, and said, "If any of us manage to survive, look for Paliski.

There we will meet." Paliski was a good man; a Polish gentile; one of the few we could trust.

We climbed into one of the wagons, where a young Jewish man asked us to follow him. The heat was hellish. About 150 men were crammed in that car together. We could hardly breathe. Desperate and on the verge of fainting, we shouted:

"Water! Water!"

What we received were instead bullets. From the top of the train, the Nazis shot at us, demanding silence.

A young man who had asked us to follow him had a hacksaw. With it, he began to cut, until he managed to file the bars of the window. It was small, hardly big enough for human beings to pass through; at least that is what I thought at first. We all helped each other to get through that small gap. We passed through that window, which would take us to freedom or death. We knew that it was risky, and we were faced with a real Russian roulette. Some broke bones in the fall; a slow and painful death. Some had better luck and died in one blow against a tree or pole or against the ground when falling. Despite those possible fates, many of us preferred to die, betting on freedom, rather than to go like lambs to the slaughter of the Nazis, passive and melancholy, defeated at last by horror.

That is how I escaped the train of my destiny. Launched like a projectile, like a battered object, rushed by the instinct of survival. I remember the feeling of being lifted up by those unknown men, the emptiness in my stomach being thrown through that little space, the never-ending flight in my memory, the painful fall, the blow to my head, and the unconsciousness. It was like a dream to hear the train moving away forever, towards never.

Once I was able to sit up, I wandered in a daze. I stumbled over corpses, with dozens of wounded people in pain and asking for help. I walked without knowing the direction of my departure. I suddenly became aware that I was alone in the world. All my loved ones had died or traveled to death without return.

I came across a tree
and felt the urgent need to embrace it,
perhaps to feel that I was still alive,
that not everything on this earth had disappeared,
that nature still stands among such human misery.
Perhaps I wanted the tree to transmit its strength
impervious to that apocalyptic scene,
of bodies strewn on the ground,
some already free of horror,
others on their way to a
painful and terrible
liberation.

That moment would mark my life forever. I have never left that nameless place, hugging that tree forever. All my life, I have stayed there. From that moment, everything that I had experienced came down to that moment, just like water inevitably seeking the eye of the whirlpool.

And after so much time, I was finally able to shout:

"MY G-D, WHAT HAVE I DONE?"

Chapter V

The Long Night of the Flight

I

Run, brother,
for the shadows chase us.
The world, in flight, is touched
by the wounding lights of dawn.

Bodies have left their materiality
in broken mirrors of light,
and the dawn's red gaze
strives not to drain
our memories.

I run, Brother.
Nothing left behind.
Everything has gone,
forever leaving behind
roads without steps,
efforts without struggles and
places without corners
in which to take shelter.

45

Do not stop the march, Brother.
From this moment on
our destiny will be no more than flight.
There will never be anything to call our own.
Without a country, we will wander,
without a land, without a home,
without moons or suns
to shine down at us.

Today
they took everything from us, forever.
I run, brother.
We will never stop running.

II

I walked for days, directionless, avoiding the roads. At some houses, I asked for food, so as not to starve. I knew that getting close enough to ask for food was a great risk. There were many Polish gentiles who, out of fear of the Germans or contempt for our people, would sell us in the vilest way: for a kilogram of sugar, or the fragile certainty of taking safety from our danger.

Perhaps
they believe that
feeding the wolves
with the flesh of the Jew
will satisfy its beastly appetite,
its insatiable thirst for blood.
But, as I would later understand,
hunger is stronger than fear.

After a long journey, I finally arrived at the house of Mr. Paliski, the Polish man in whom my mother placed her trust. He was a family friend who traded in wheat and had done business with my brother-in-law, Zeilig, before the war.

Paliski received me without hesitation and in his house I waited, sick with anguish and fear, but also with hope for the arrival of one of my own: my mother, my brothers, or sister. I prayed that they had been saved, that this horror was no more than a nightmare from which we would awaken. Every second, every minute, every hour, and day, was an insurmountable torture. Nobody arrived. And little by little, my hopes faded. Then, after nine days my brother Yankel arrived at the meeting place.

My brother Yankel had also been thrown from that train, which was taking us to death; the same one that ended up taking our loved ones, the same one that would live forever in my nightmares.

My brother had finally arrived, but with him came the imperative need to move, to leave, to continue our aimless wandering. My dear brother had traveled many kilometers looking for the house of that good man who would help us, but along the way, he did it in the most indiscreet way possible. He asked everyone he met for directions to Paliski's house. It was to be expected, then, that many people would know that Paliski would be willing to protect some Jews in flight. It was not difficult to assess the situation. Now, faced with the danger that would ruin the life of our benefactor and our own lives by that indiscretion, we made the decision to leave the house immediately.

And so, for two years,
we lived in hiding in the forest,
enduring the terrible winter cold,
the ruthless rains.

Living with the chilling fear
of being captured by the Germans
or handed over by the Poles.

I had many experiences and made many sacrifices during those two years. The experiences were never erased from my mind and left eternal traces in my soul. Our lives, and those of all other Jews, were pushed to the limit. What inner strength managed to keep us alive? Was it G-d? I can hardly believe in Him when I think of the lives that were lost, or the pain we endured, in so much injustice and brutality. Could I believe in Him, at the thought of my mother, my brothers, and sister; my nephews and nieces; our blood spilled mercilessly by our enemies?

However, I know it would have been impossible for us to survive without the determination of some superior force, to preserve our lives.

The human soul is perhaps
the greatest mystery.
There are so many masks,
layers that society obligates us to use,
when the truth of our nature
stays concealed
and hidden from others.

Most do not have the bravery
to confront the darkness
even in their own abyss.
We would be terrified
if we could peer into the soul of a person
we have always believed we knew.

We would die of horror
or go crazy

OY MAME! OY MAME!

even in the presence of our own soul,
stripped of its masks and deception.

We endured the apocalypse, the end of time. Society was shattered, and the barbarians, enemies of culture, man, and his thousand-year-old heritage, attacked everything. It turned us into animals.

This society in ruins was unable to maintain its festive masks. Full of horror, we could see the unfathomable abyss of the soul. Most were monsters thirsty for blood, for power. Many, we discovered, were capable of anything just to survive. But some showed an angel's face, where the goodness of G-d was reflected. They were few, but we owe them our lives. One of them was Boleslav Lubian.

We called him Bolek. He was a Polish gentile and a family friend. He had worked with Jews for years and knew the Jewish community of the area. He had five children: Maniek, the eldest, Tadeusz, Chanek, Yanina, and Stefan, the youngest of whom was only 6 years old. That family was our salvation at times when death haunted us, whispering in our ears strange melodies that I have forgotten, but I feel since then. There are many memories of those harrowing days for us that have to do with Bolek and his family.

How many times had our lives been saved in the Bolek stables? At night, when we could not stand the cold, we went to his house and in his stables, next to the cows, we managed to warm up. For many nights, the warmth of those animals was our salvation, as the cold demanded its right to kill us, to erase us forever from that bitter and indifferent land of our tragedy.

I remember one time the Germans came to Bolek's house and were about to find us hiding in the attic.

In order to survive, Maniek used to steal sheep. Bolek's eldest son was, like his father, an excellent human being. But the good young man had to steal sheep and sell them for some money to survive the war. He would bring the sheep to his father's stables.

49

The problem was that the house, located in a wasteland, a sort of tundra, was the only house for many miles around. The tracks of the sheep would undoubtedly guide the Germans there, in search of the lost animals. I could sense it and I remember reprimanding the young man:

"Your imprudence will bring the Germans here."

And so it was.

When we heard the Germans approaching, my brother and I went up to the attic of the stable and tried to cover ourselves with straw. Of course, the hiding place and the straw would be an absolutely ridiculous and insufficient disguise if the German soldiers suspected us and went up to the place to check. They did.

With a ladder, they went up and looked far away, into the distance, past our straw-covered crevice. We were right there. We could see them, and our breathing stopped. I remember feeling utterly lost. There was no way they would not see us. That would be the end for us and for Bolek and his family.

But some miracle made those men missed us. I have never been able to explain how those men did not see us right under their noses. It was as if a superior force had made us invisible, to save our lives.

Or are we no more than puppets of life, of history;
fragile leaves
whisked away by the wind?

It seems that G-d had other plans for us. This time too, death passed us by.

That was not the only time I felt the certainty that our time had come, that our agony would come to a sudden stop when we would be discovered, and the Germans would end up killing us, right there.

Before this certainty that faced us with the most ungraspable of the depths, I do not remember thinking about the future of Bolek if they found us in his stable. Maybe he could have sworn he did not know we were there, that he was outraged by our presence among his cows. Then his luck would have been left in the hands of the murderers, subject to the whim of the highest-ranking officer.

I have never stopped thinking about the kindness of those people. They risked their lives to save us. They gave us shelter when we could not survive.

Then there was Yanina, Bolek's only daughter. She was so afraid. She used to beg her father to give us over to the Germans or get us out of there. She knew perfectly well what their fate would be if the Germans could prove that they were hiding Jews in his house. I overheard her discussions with a deep resentment. But with the passage of time, I came to understand her terror. But what would have become of us, and to many other Jews, had there not been people who overcame their fear to help us?

Among Polish children, there was a tradition of raising rabbits. The children used to visit the neighboring houses to see their friends' rabbits. Stefan, who at that time was only 6 years old, was a charming and intelligent child. Despite being so small, he understood our situation and the danger that our presence in his house meant for us all.

One day he came and said, "Today my friends will come to see the rabbits, so you must not even breathe. I will try to show the rabbits quickly so that my friends leave soon, and you can come out of hiding easily."

No doubt his father had taught him well.

Another time, one of Bolek's sons asked me to teach him to speak Yiddish. Bolek heard him and said, "Why do you want to speak Yiddish? Don't you understand? There are no Jews with whom to speak!"

Sometimes, when Bolek felt that our presence was particularly dangerous, he would talk to us and ask us to leave. We agreed. But when night came, we had no choice but to return to our benefactor's stables, without him knowing. Where else could we go?

And in the darkness of the stable, I would think about the others, about those of us who had not been able to get off that fateful train. I could not escape the question:

"Why, G-d? Why did you allow all this to happen?"

I remember a particular Jewish preacher. Before the war, he would go from town to town, like an ancient prophet. In Yiddish, he would warn us about our behavior and the consequences it would bring on us:

"Fire will burn in the cities. Women do not go to the mikvah[26], Jews change their names. Our people are assimilating and falling into sin. The result of all this will be destruction, pain, death."

And I would wonder if this man, whom many thought crazy, could have a point. So many things went through our heads, but above all the immense desire to preserve life. That was the inner fire that made us keep fighting when it seemed that everything was lost; that made us draw strength when our legs and arms refused to move.

One day we learned that a group of nine Jews was hiding in the forest. The desire to be with our fellows prompted us to look for them. We arrived at night where they were hiding, but a hunch alerted me. There is a saying that goes, 'There is no heart traitor to his master.' I have always believed in this. My heart has shown me the way many times, it has taken me to safe places away from death.

---

[26] Mikvah: Jewish ritual bath.

I told my brother, "Yankel, my heart tells me that we are not safe here."

But Yankel only replied, "I stay here, and you will go".

And so, I returned to my hiding place. The next morning, I learned that that same night a group of Poles had found the Jews hidden in the forest. They pleaded with their capturers not to deliver them. But the Poles did not listen to their pleas. They gave them to the Germans, who mercilessly fired on those fugitives. When I learned of that slaughter, I felt my heart sink from my chest.

I remember saying to myself with desolation, "Now I really am alone in the world."

Desperate, I began walking, but close to my village a man told me, "I saw your brother."

That news filled me with hope and, eagerly following the directions that the man had given me, I went to look for my brother, begging G-d to let me find him alive. This time, too, G-d heard my prayers. I was able to find my brother, who was badly suffering from swollen feet and a bullet wound. Fortunately, he had managed to escape the massacre, but a bullet went through his hip. Thankfully, it did not lodge in his body. But the wound had to be healed as soon as possible. And so, I carried my brother on my back, since his legs would not respond, and he was very weak.

When we arrived at Bolek's house, little Stefan ran into town to buy the hydrogen peroxide which we used to cure Yankel.

My brother managed to recover from that wound. He always explained how he had managed to escape by running in a zigzag, as fast as he could, and how bullets buzzed in his ears like fateful bees. Again, a miracle had saved my brother Yankel from death.

On one occasion I experienced something similar when a German saw me and ordered me to stop. My immediate reaction was to run and the soldier shot more bullets at me than there are hairs on my head.

There were many massacres like that, from which my brother and I escaped. I remember a large group of Jews — there were 49 of our people. They were murdered by the Germans and buried in a cave. Among them was a man named Hertzog, whose children managed to survive. After the Germans were defeated and had left Poland, the two Hertzog brothers set out to find the body of their father, who had hidden three gold coins in a jockstrap on his thigh. While searching in the cave they found the coins and thus they recognized the corpse of their father among so many.

Many difficult moments made us strong. There is the feeling of having lost sensibility, no longer being human. The war turns everyone into monsters a little, and life acquires another meaning.

I remember a Jewish boy who tried to survive in the forest with us, hiding wherever he could to escape our enemies, Poles and Germans. The young man got a bullet wound in his hand. The damage a single bullet can cause is incredible. Usually, one thinks of the dead, but those who survive suffer terribly from the destructive power of bullets. Without the necessary means, we knew that we could not do much to save that boy's hand. We made the decision immediately and without doubt; we cut off his hand and used our urine to clean the wound and prevent it from becoming infected.

There was another Polish man who also took a risk to help our people. This man gathered a group of forty Jews and hid them in a house. He had a big heart and wanted to protect his fellow human beings from death. I am not sure what happened to him and that group of Jews.

Paliski, Bolek, and that Polish man, who helped those forty Jews, represent the small percentage of Polish gentiles who were supportive and humane to Jews in that terrible time. However, the vast majority of them seemed to become our executioners. We were as

Polish as they were. Our ancestors had arrived in Poland a thousand years before. How could anyone think of us as foreigners? But that's how it was. The Poles sold us in exchange for sugar. They gave us to the Germans to earn their sympathy or simply killed us to steal our properties and our goods. That was the harsh reality. How might things have been different, had the Poles treated us like their compatriots, their brothers? Where was the human being willing to help his neighbor? In these two years of war, we learned of the evil of many Polish gentiles and their hatred towards the Jews.

Once, along with two other Jews, I went to the house of a Pole we knew, hoping he would feed us. We were willing to ask or steal. We knew there was a lot of risk in this, but hunger is more powerful than fear. When we arrived at the home, we knew from the smell that they were baking bread. The Pole let us in and gave us some freshly baked bread. But he had a plan. Without us noticing, he sent one of his sons to call the group of Poles who were in charge of hunting and killing Jews. Suddenly, the house was surrounded. My two companions managed to escape, but I fell into the hands of the murderers. They made me leave the house and gave me a shovel to dig my own grave. Once again, I felt that my end had arrived. But one of my companions, who had managed to escape, started shooting at them. The Poles worried, even more, when I told them that we were not alone and that a group of Jewish partisans would come to liberate me. In a moment of uncertainty, I took the opportunity to escape, saving my life once more.

Desperate as our situation was, we fell into the hands of a known thief. This was a Polish gentile who made a living from theft and deception. It was even rumored that he had killed someone. He offered to protect us if we helped him in his illegal and shady trades. It was then that two other Jews and I dedicated ourselves to the theft of cows and pigs. My brother, fortunately, had nothing to do with this.

Once the robber gave us the order to go to the border to steal horses. We explained that this was impossible. We did not have the proper means to move, the roads were dangerous, especially for the Jews, and the footprints of the horses in the snow would have given us away.

Then the man told us, "Go steal and kill pigs. Bring me the pigs in the canal to freeze their meat."

So, we decided to go steal and kill pigs, as the thief demanded. I remember the first time we hung the pig with a rope. When we killed it and cut it open, we realized that it was a sow and that its stomach was full of unborn piglets.

Several times, we brought pigs on the canal to that Pole who claimed to be our protector. Once the three of us took part of a pig to sell it on our own. When I got the profit, I wanted to share it among the three, but my good companions told me, "No. That money will be for you and your brother. When the war passes, we also will all be brothers and help each other."

Unfortunately, those good men did not manage to survive the war and we never got the chance to pay them back.

When the thief finally decided that we got enough meat, he ordered us to get potatoes. When we asked him for tools to extract the potatoes the man told us, "The potatoes should be extracted with your fingernails. If you use another tool the taste of the potato is not the same."

We had worked for that man for many days, plucking potatoes with our painful, blood-stained fingernails.

When we finally finished our work, the thief shouted, "You imbeciles! They saw you coming here. Now you must leave because if the Germans come and find you in my house you will have caused the end of me."

That man used us. He took advantage of our misery and vulnerability to exploit us and then throw us into the street to our fate. His behavior was the rule among the Polish, not the exception. Our people lived through the unspeakable. Among the groups of Jews in hiding were women who had small children, newborns. Many mothers had to drown their own children so that their cries would not betray the others. How could a mother survive after this? I will never tire of asking these things. After experiencing all this, it is nothing short of a miracle that we were not driven into absolute madness, into the shadows of our own souls, the blindness of the soul and the mind. And yet we are here. We managed to survive one of the most terrifying episodes in the history of humanity, and our existence may be proof that the spirit of the human being is invincible.

Chapter VI

Frieda

I

Apart from shadow and pain,
Frieda,
there is silence,
the destructive hands of winter
and the depth of your gaze
when the day rests.

Nothing really exists,
Frieda,
Existence is so absolute
that in the end, it involves us
in storm and tragedy,
just like the spring
and your voice, overwhelming the silence.

Everything is a fate of memories;
fierce horses that chase us from dreams
and have learned to leap over boundaries
and to lurk in the living room

where everyone talks about
the triviality of the day and the vanities.
For us, for Frieda,
They stopped making sense long ago.

When the sun rose again,
after so much night.
When the world regained its color
and things regained their natural smells
and the tastes of their soul and wonder,
when the cold seemed to give a pause
and the warmth started to comfort us from within,
you were there, resuming the world,
helping me to start
after all the failures.

II

The two years we spent in the woods hiding from the Germans and their Polish minions were an eternity for us. They were not two years but all our past and future lives bleeding before our eyes at every moment. On one hand, our loved ones never leave us. Hope, like a dagger in our side, forces us to believe that at any moment our loved ones could appear somewhere, lost in some city, hidden in some house, forest or basement. Our future also passed before our eyes since the present was only the constant threat of never having a future in which to cement our dreams. My soul deceived me by hoping that, like my brother Yankel, my mother and my brothers would arrive at the house of the good Paliski, following the plan drawn up by her. Then they would ask Paliski for us and, happy that we were alive, they would look for us until we met. How many times have I dreamed of that encounter?

Time, in reality, is an eternal present. I heard this once: the past does not exist, it is only in our memories, a falsified creation of nostalgia for the lost; the future does not exist, creation of our desire or fear. If the only real time is an eternal present, they took away time and with it, life. I must admit, then, that somehow we were dead, and G-d almighty gave us a truce to continue.

When the war ended, the hope of finding one of our own led us to Lodz, a city to which thousands of Jews came after wandering all over Poland; even repatriated Polish Jews came, mainly from Russia. At this time, because Warsaw had been almost completely destroyed, Lodz became the temporary capital of Poland; the possibility of moving the capital permanently was even considered, but this idea did not have much support. In 1948, the reconstruction of Warsaw and its rehabilitation as capital would begin. Like us, the thousands of refugees who arrived daily in Lodz expected to find relatives or acquaintances. Poland was then a Dantesque refugee camp. The apocalyptic environment remained engraved in an indelible way in all the human beings who lived through the tragedy. I know that is the way it is. It could not be otherwise.

We lived out in the open, sleeping in stables, caves, or under the sky when the weather was clearer. In the city we needed a safe place to shelter, a place to spend the night without dangers. Lodz offered several possibilities, and only this fact was, for us, a breakthrough. One of these options was to find an unoccupied house, in any state, and take possession of it. Another option was to find a relative, friend, or even an acquaintance that, in an act of unconditional kindness, would give you the opportunity to stay in a space where he or she already lived. It was very common to find small housing spaces occupied by several families.

So, my brother and I found an unoccupied house and decided to take it as our temporary home, our first since our family tragedy began. But even though the war had passed, our hunger had not. We did not have any income and we needed to feed ourselves so that our hardship and struggle would count for something. We could not starve now, just when the sun seemed to start shining again. Walking through Lodz we arrived at a small restaurant that a fellow Jew had opened. No doubt the man had also suffered all the hardships of war, persecution, and most likely, the loss of his loved ones. He must understand our desperation, I thought.

Betting on that, I approached to propose the following deal, "Please, we need to eat. Give my brother only broth without meat. I promise you, as soon as I earn some money, I'll pay you back."

I did not dare to ask for meat because I knew that he was also poor and would not have much to share. But the good man accepted and gave my brother and me broth to drink.

G-d was so good to me that, when I was in the small restaurant, a Russian man came, selling a type of thick cloth that served as a boot and jacket lining. I recognized a good opportunity to earn some money and I approached the Russian to propose to be his partner in the sale of the fabric.

He asked me, "How much money do you have to support the partnership?"

I have no money. But if you entrust me with part of the merchandise, I will go to Warsaw, a city I know very well, and I assure you that I will sell the cloth."

"Do not think that I will give you the fabric without having a guarantee on your part."

"As a guarantee, my brother Yankel will stay with you while I go to Warsaw and return with the money from the sale. What do you think?"

The man agreed and my brother stayed with him during the hours I needed to sell the cloth in the ruined capital and return, happy to have made my first successful post-war business. I gave the Russian the money he deserved, paid back the good restaurant owner for the broth that my brother had eaten, and in the evening we were able to return to that restaurant to ask, this time, for two soup plates with meat and vegetables.

I will never forget the taste of that hot soup, clean and completely ours. In the following days, I repeated that business with the Russian cloth seller. I was able to earn a little money that allowed us to eat and start covering our basic needs.

Lodz was a whirlpool, a post-apocalyptic city where people fought for survival and, among the thousands of previously established inhabitants and the thousands of refugees who arrived daily, searched for relatives or acquaintances with which to support themselves and share the misery and loneliness. Destiny led us to find a paternal cousin named Rosie, who was married to Yosel Beker. For us, finding someone we knew was an immense happiness. We embraced each other enthusiastically and, with unbearable pain, we narrated our respective tragedies. She told us how they had managed to save their lives by escaping to Russia, and how after the war ended, they returned to Poland by train.

The details of her story exhausted, my cousin told me, "On the train from Russia there was a Jewish family that was in refuge there during the war. They have a daughter that will be 19 years old now. She could be a good shidduch for you."

I thought that everything I had to lose had already been lost, so I agreed to accompany my cousin to the *lage*[27], called Shvienti Yacuba. We would visit the family and I would see the girl they had told me about. We arrived, my cousin presented me decently, and I greeted and saw her. Her name was Frieda. She was a thin girl with beautiful features and she was 11 years younger than me. I did not need a second visit. I knew that she should be in my life from that moment.

---

[27] Center for the displaced.

Between my cousin, my brother, and I, we began to plan a strategy to get to the house of my future in-laws and make a good impression. What worried me the most was that Frieda's parents were extremely religious. Both had all the appearance of Orthodox Jews. My concern had to do with the serious doubts I had then that have accompanied me all my life. Had G-d saved us from death on multiple occasions? I knew that was it, I felt it. But at the time I was tormented by so many questions: *Why did G-d not save the others? Why did G-d allow the enemies of His people to be satisfied with eating the flesh and drinking the blood of the lambs?* Faith, for me, was a great ambiguity. I had time to walk with my head uncovered, but I knew that I could not present myself like that to Frieda's parents; I had to make the right impression. I presented myself before them with a brimmed hat and I was dressed as modestly as possible.

It seemed that the hat helped. They allowed me to see Frieda, the woman who would be my companion for the next 65 years.

III

F rieda was born on November 4th, 1927, in Narol, Poland; at 2 Ulitza Mnieska street. Her parents were Sure Goldberg, nee Grinberg, and Moishe Leib Goldberg. They had several brothers and sisters who also had children. It was a large family that disappeared almost entirely during the Holocaust.

Frieda was the youngest of six siblings: Guiche, Peiru, Mote, Sender, Ruju, the latter three known as Uncle Max, Dod Sender, and Doda Ruju. She completed primary school in a public school very close to her house. Unlike what I endured; Frieda had beautiful memories of this time in school. She always remembers her headmaster, Yan Brenczko, and her best friends Marisha Zaremska and Charna Korman. In school, Frieda learned to speak, read, and write perfect

Polish. To this day she surprises me with her remarkable language skills, as she speaks Yiddish, Polish, Russian, and Spanish.

When the war came to Poland in September 1939, the city where my wife was born was devastated by enemy fire. The inhabitants were forced to flee and her family went to Lemberg.

However, the family did not stay together. Guiche and Peiru, already married, traveled with their respective families to Rave Ruske[28]. Their husbands were from this city, in the Lemberg area. Guiche was married to Beirish Gurfinkel and they had three children: Mindale, Frimit, and Solomon. Peiru was married to Moshe Shpritze and they had only one son named Yankele.

In Lemberg, Frieda and her family lived at Rulkienska Street 19. They did not stay there for longer than a few months since the Russians came to occupy the area. They arrived one day in the morning and ordered the local population to leave immediately. This illustrates the pain, uncertainty, and unpredictability that filled so many lives during those years.

The Russians took them out of the city and they did not ask where they were taking them or why. They traveled for six weeks in a train made for the transport of pigs. The Russians gave them sausages, which my father-in-law forbade eating because they were pork. They slept on the bare floor of the wagons. But they were not pressed or shot or starved or taken to their deaths. How different was that train that took my Frieda, from mine which took us to Treblinka, that ever-recurring train from which Yankel and I were thrown?

Finally, they arrived at the Ustyug station. From there they were transported by truck to a town called Sharya[29], in Russia, where they were taken to the barracks. So vivid was that experience that my

---

[28] Rava-Ruska, Ukraine.
[29] Sharya, Kostroma Oblast.

wife remembers exactly the address of that refuge where they lived for three years:

*Vologodskaia Oblast Nikolsky Raion Murrokudanski
Lesapunkt, barrack number 3.*

Work was done in this place. My brothers-in-law sawed wood to be sent to Moscow across the river. My in-laws and my sister-in-law worked in the kitchen of the barracks. They worked this hard so that Frieda could go to school. It was there that she learned to speak, read, and write perfect Russian.

My wife's family was liberated from this work camp near Sharya in 1943. They immediately moved to Nikolsk. In this city, my brothers-in-law were drafted into the army and transferred to the Polish border. My brother-in-law Sender was shot and left crippled for life. They could never extract the bullet. My sister-in-law also worked for the military, in another way. Her job was to use special ovens to dehydrate the potatoes for the soldiers' consumption. While the others worked, Frieda went to school and learned. Those years were happy for her despite everything. She did not feel the persecution or the hatred that my brother and I felt; she did not feel the murderous anti-semitism that we suffered. While I would like to forget, she fondly remembers her companions at the time: Zina Popova, Voronina Olga, Cudrisnka Ttasia, and Romanofna Nina, the best student at the school and her best friend. When we went to Israel, Frieda was able to see another of her companions: Shainld Zisman.

Frieda also has bitter memories, of course, like that of her friend Kusniatsova Nina, who died of starvation in the war.

Frieda's life in Nikolsk was easier than in Sharya. The climate was warmer and they lived much more comfortably, in a small but cozy little room where they even had a kitchen. Her diet was comprised almost entirely of potatoes. By then, Sender was working in the only town bakery.

When the war finished in 1945, my future wife and her family left Nikolsk and were transferred to Berezovka[30], 80 kilometers from Odessa. My in-laws were transferred to Worms[31], but Frieda, who continued studying, stayed in Berezovka with her friend Shaindl Zisman.

Frieda lived with a family at 4 Rosa Luxemburg St. Every Sunday she took the train and then walked to arrive at her parents' house in Worms. Her mother gave her food for the whole week and Frieda would return to continue her routine as a student.

The situation in Berezovka was interesting. The Russians housed many Jews in houses that had belonged to an important German colony once. After the war, the Germans were stripped of their properties and exiled from the city. After a year, Frieda and her family finally returned to their homeland. It was the year 1946 when Frieda, her parents, her two brothers, and her sister Rachel finally left Russia. The journey to Poland lasted four weeks by train until they crossed the border. At each station, they would go down and find out the directions of the trains and take the one that would bring them closer to their homeland.

Even though Frieda did not live through the horror that my brother and I witnessed during the war, she and her family did not pass through those dark times unscathed. Guiche and Peiru, Frieda's older sisters, were murdered along with their families. They were living in Lemberg when the Germans arrived there to arrest all the Jews that lived there and send them to concentration camps. Upon arrival in Poland, Frieda's family searched for Guiche and Peiru. They asked their relatives and friends about them and their families. When they finally arrived in Lemberg they understood what had happened and mourned their dead like the millions of other human beings who had endured that never-ending nightmare.

---

[30] Berevizka, Berevizka, Odessa, Ukraine.
[31] Vinogradnoye, Berevizka, Odessa, Ukraine.

When they arrived in Lemberg, a Polish gentile allowed them to live in his basement. This good man had a bakery. Because the city was full of soldiers, both Polish and Russian, Frieda's parents and brothers forbade her to go out into the street. At that time, she was 18 years old and it was logical that they feared for her safety.

Understandably however, Frieda was bored and eager to go out, to see people in the streets, to feel the sun and the breeze on her skin. She begged her father and brothers to let her out and they finally accepted. Destiny led Frieda to meet a kind, dignified Polish soldier on the street, who greeted her kindly. When he opened his mouth, she could see a gold tooth, which immediately led her to recognize the nice young man. It was her cousin Itzack, who had lost his wife and children in the war. He lived in a beautiful house at 14 Sikstutska Street, in Lwow. He generously offered his house to the family of my future wife and they settled there until they left for Lodz.

Frida's parents learned that there was a significantly sized Jewish population in Lodz, so they made the decision to move there. Like many other Jews at this time, they managed to survive largely thanks to the help of the American Jewish Joint Distribution Committee and Refugee Aid, commonly known as the Joint, which was responsible for providing clothing and food to Jewish survivors of the war in Europe.

When they reached Lodz, they went to a *lage* in the city. It was precisely there where our cousin introduced us. After three months of getting to know each other, we got married. It was March 19, 1947. The wedding plans were simple and humble, because of our circumstances. The permission to get married under the Jewish rules was given to us by the congregation on Zajodnia Street 66. We were, obviously, extremely poor. The war had left us nearly nothing, apart from the most important thing: life and the hope of being able to live it anew, reborn from the ashes. My dear Frieda did not have adequate clothes for the ceremony, so her brother Sender borrowed a dress from a friend. The marriage took place where I lived, 15 Cegielniana Street, at the bottom of an alley.

I remember that an entire chicken was prepared for the wedding feast. Frieda and I fasted the whole day in preparation for such an important ceremony, according to the religious custom, and we longed to share that chicken between us. It was insufficient for all the guests and the hunger shared between them. But in the end, neither she nor I could even taste the chicken, as the guests devoured it before we had the chance. However, we did enjoy some bread and a *leikach*, a dry cake traditional for wedding meals.

Frieda was still very young and therefore inexperienced in all the chores of the house. All those years she had devoted herself to studying, while her brothers and sister had carried the burden and responsibility of helping their parents in the maintenance of the home. When we got married, she was tremendously worried about not being able to manage the chores of the house like a true housewife.

Naturally, for Frieda, it was a huge surprise when I asked her if my brother Yankel could live with us for some time. I know that for Frieda it was not easy to confront this strange family situation.

My wife, however, accepted my request. She has always been a brilliant person and she immediately understood that, given the circumstances, it would be very hard for my brother to remain totally alone in the world.

How could I part with his company?
He was the only other survivor from my family.
He had lived by my side
through the most terrible moments
of persecution, hunger, and fear.
What would have become of me without him?
What would have happened to him without me?

We stayed in Lodz until 1949, because Yankel and I had started a sandal factory, which we sold to some shops and from house to house. But although the war was over and the Germans were gone, Polish hatred and persecution continued. The news indicated that the massacre of Jews had returned. We did not want to endure that nightmare again, so we decided to leave Poland, a land that had ceased to be ours a long time ago. Because the war had revealed the truth; that land had never belonged to us. We Jews were still the same nomads after 1,000 years.

So, we made the difficult decision to leave everything in Lodz and traveled to Bielsk, a Polish border city. It was easy to cross the border into Czechoslovakia from there. It was a brief stop, though, since Frieda's parents had been living in Munich for some time, in Gräfelfing. From Czechoslovakia, we went to Austria and from there to Germany, where our daughter Chana was born in the University Clinic at 11 Maistraße Munich. We lived in Germany until 1952.

Chapter VII

Beyond the Sea

I

The sea is unfathomable. Everyone knows it. Mystery spreads from its depths until it seeps into everything on earth.

To cross the sea is to start over,
to reach a place
where dawn greets no homeland every morning,
a place that has been among your dreams
always, secretly
without anyone knowing
without its aroma invading the consciousness
but instead pervading dreams
from the very origin of scent and desire.

Beyond the sea are life, freedom, and hope.
Crossing the sea means seeing objects from another perspective.
It means to unveil the back of the moon;
to see the other side of the mirror.
Crossing the sea means listening to all the voices
that were seemingly silenced

but that, we know, have gone somewhere,
bleeding out.

Beyond the sea, life must be possible,
because here death was so possible
that we all became prisoners.

II

After all we had experienced, for us, Europe meant death, tragedy, and helplessness.

How could we be sure
that night would not return?
In that land of our childhoods,
that country branded in our bones,
our loved ones remained,
after they had been snatched away
as though they were a plague that might
contaminate the air.

Poland ceased to belong to us because it is not the hospitable land that gives you shelter and food. When the wolves arrived, that ungrateful land abandoned us; our neighbors became our enemies, persecutors, and informers. The people we always thought we knew, with whom we bought and sold, the people we greeted in the streets, the families of the children who had joined in our games and our poverty; they turned against us and watched us die without flinching. Many even took up the weapons that killed us or led the pack to our shelters.

How could we remain in a land that had forgotten us?

Upon leaving Poland we saw the same scenes, the same pain, the same fear, the same trails of suffering. The smell of blood permeated everything we looked at. It was like witnessing everything again. We had to get away, to look for new lives and new hopes.

Most of us dreamt of escaping from everything. Maybe this hope is inevitable. But time has taught me that no matter where you go, you can never truly escape what torments you. Nothing ever leaves you. All your pain, tragedy, hatred, and revenge remain in your soul and you must bear them as a condemnation wherever you go.

We had thought a lot about our future, and we had everything ready to travel to Israel, where my wife's parents had already settled. Now we had one extra responsibility and motivation; our daughter Chany, whose name in Yiddish is Chana, just like my beloved mother. She deserved to grow and live in a better world than that in which we lived. This was our main legacy.

She would not be humiliated or persecuted or murdered, like we were. I felt responsible for my family and would not allow anything or anyone to harm them.

My brother Yankel, who I wanted to have by my side forever, would travel with us, because leaving him would have meant reliving our tragedy, losing my parents and siblings, staying now and forever detached from my past and from my blood.

We sent our *bagash* [32] to Israel, which contained two motorcycles, two bicycles, a sewing machine, and some important items to start a new life in Israel. Although, substantially, what we sent may not seem like much, for us it was a great portion of our possessions and the possibility of getting ahead in the nascent Jewish state.

But G-d did not want us to make that trip. Upon learning of our decision to travel, my father-in-law reached out to us and told us

---

[32] Personal belongings in bags.

how hard life in Israel was at that time. He told us about the hardships and difficulties that the immigrants coming to our land with the same hopes and dreams had to endure.

In light of such discouraging news, our futures were redirected towards America. It had always seemed to us that America was the United States. Little did we actually know about this vast and wonderful continent. My wife's brother lived in the United States, so the plans were to travel there.

However, laws that sought to regulate the arrival of European immigrants (mainly Jews) grew increasingly rigid. Not a long time had passed since the end of the war, and a devastated Europe, physically and emotionally, saw millions of its men and women leave to someplace where they could heal their deep wounds.

The three of us agreed that the struggles of moving to America were almost insuperable. Our hopes were extinguished like candles in the wind. The option of moving to the United States was rejected, but without losing heart I began to investigate other possibilities. The feeling of not recognizing what your home is and feeling that there is no place in the world for you and your loved ones is indescribably painful.

A friend who knew of my search for a new life abroad mentioned to me that there was a South American country that was not placing any limits or restrictions on the arrival of Jews. That country was Bolivia, one of the Andean countries of South America.

The friend who traveled to Bolivia arranged the visas that enabled us to leave Europe. We had to pay to obtain this visa, and when it finally arrived, the four of us embarked on an overseas journey that would last us a month. The ship took us first to Italy, where we made a technical stop and had the chance to go down to the port.

The first American country we stopped at was Brazil. We stayed there for a few days before following the course towards our final destination.

With us came our hope, but also our uncertainty. I knew we were strong and enterprising. If we had been able to survive the hell that is war, surely nothing could beat us now. But we were venturing into the unknown and that is always a cause for anxiety.

I remember the feeling when I arrived in La Paz. We took the train to a city that was completely different from everything we knew. Its altitude of over 3,600 meters above sea level makes breathing heavy and difficult, and the cold, accompanied by the dry air, provoked in us new sensations, like having always our lips parted.

We were not the only Jews to arrive in Bolivia. In the city of La Paz, we were received by Jews who were already living there. The Jewish community of La Paz had grown immensely in the period after the war. The majority of its members had arrived from Poland and Germany. My family (my wife, my daughter Chana and my brother Yankel) began to become part of a larger family. We soon found friends and true brothers in our fellow European Jews, immigrants like us, exiles just like us, who had suffered persecution and death, just like us. They were people of solidarity, willing to help and share their few possessions and their poverty. Those good men and women were willing to cry with us, comfort us and rid us of all the terrors we had suffered. Some soothed the pain by sharing their own sad stories; others chose to maintain absolutely silent about what they had experienced; a few maintained a silence that would accompany them to the grave; others, with each passing decade, agreed to share a little more about their experiences of the Holocaust.

Little by little, we began to adapt to Bolivian society, to its food, its customs, and its culture. It was all so different from Europe, as if it were a world of its own. However, it is beyond doubt that the locals were good and generous people. The Bolivians, who at first seemed distant and silent, chewing coca leaves all day, proved to be good people with big hearts. Most accepted us genuinely, although there was never a lack of people to remind us, in a derogatory way, that we were Jews. But the place was safe and its people were safe; like a balm we needed to soothe our wounds. I say "soothe" because I have never been able to calm the pain of those years in Poland.

The agony of my loved ones' cries from that train
which took away much of my heart and my soul,
has always remained with me,
leaving only my dreams, my vigil,
and guilt like an anchor on my back.

We rented a small house in the famous Miraflores neighborhood. This site owes its fame mainly to the Hernando Siles stadium, the largest in the country and one of the highest altitude professional stadiums in the world. On the outskirts of the stadium, every night, we saw the Cholas selling sandwiches, anticuchos, chorizos, pork rinds, silpanchos. Our neighbors were good people who always guided us and helped us adjust to life in La Paz as soon as possible.

One of the neighbors that I remember with the greatest affection is Mr. Morales. He was an educated man, intelligent, of fine manners and sincere behavior. We always talked about the possibility of traveling to the United States. Many years later, our children having already grown up, fate led us to meet again in Washington, where he had built himself a family with his wife Tula and their children Rudy and Nena.

Although Bolivia was a hospitable country for us and people were always good and generous, a part of me did not resign myself to living there. This feeling, this hunch, led me to investigate the possibility of traveling to Brazil or Argentina. Thinking seriously about it, I learned of a lawyer who promised to obtain us nationality to travel and settle in one of these countries. However, when everything seemed ready, something ended up pushing us back. I think that, after all, Bolivia had caught us. Some magic in the goodness of its people made us cling to the land.

We arrived from Germany with some money and two sets of silver cutlery. In addition, at a stop we made in the port of Naples, I took advantage of the opportunity to buy angora coats. When I arrived in Bolivia, I exchanged one thousand dollars for Bolivian pesos and, after selling the coats and one of the sets of silverware, I managed to raise a considerable amount, for that time, of Bolivian pesos. However, very soon I learned, and in the most painful way, what hyperinflation was. The money I had obtained practically vanished because the devaluations rapidly increased the zeros. A 100 Bolivian pesos bill was converted into 100,000 pesos. My wife was terribly angry to see that I had made the mistake of exchanging my dollars for the local currency, which was so quickly devalued. I quickly made the decision to invest everything I had in merchandise, since with it I could trade and avoid devaluation.

I bought all the leather that I could in the market, and I had the shippers take the merchandise to my house, where it rested for a year. After this time, the price of the leather had increased, and I managed to sell it to recover much of the invested money. Throughout the year, while the merchandise was being revalued, I had to suffer the reproaches of my brother and my wife, who complained about the terrible smell of leather we had to live with.

In Bolivia I had several businesses, always counting on the priceless help of my brother and my wife, who never left my side. We opened a shoe store in Potosí street. It was a corner business that allowed us, with much effort and dedication, to ensure our livelihood. Then we bought a shirt factory, with which we did not have much success. This business ended with an unfortunate fire. We had to start over and found a partner we represented for many years selling fabrics from a national factory. The name of the factory was Soligno. The sale of the fabrics allowed us to ascend to the middle class and to be able to live without great limitations or great luxuries either. My wife learned to drive a truck through the difficult streets of La Paz and helped us by transporting the fabrics with which we worked.

However, some circumstances forced us to leave society aside and we dedicated ourselves to a business in the most popular neighborhood of La Paz, known as Sagarnaga, where we sold full suits, coats, and shirts. Curiously, the clothing most used by men, at least at that time, was the entire costume. This business allowed us to improve our economic situation and I was able to send my children to study.

During those years, my brother Yankel traveled to the mines of Potosí, approximately every fifteen days. His job was to sell from door to door. This effort came to strengthen our income. Potosí is a city at 4500 meters above sea level. Its climate is extremely cold and dry. When my brother returned from those trips, he usually brought with him broken lips and reddened cheeks. Many times, he was accompanied by Marina, our beloved employee, to work. Many years later I met Marina in Washington, where she lived as an American citizen with her children and husband. She told me that my brother, on those trips to Potosí, would tell her:

"We cannot eat until we sell the first item.
If we do not sell, we do not eat."

This is an example of some of the many feats that my brother and I would do to provide sustenance and some comforts to our family.

In the year 1955 my son was born, to whom we gave the same name as my father: Mortje Izrok. As Ashkenazi Jews, we often name our children after ancestors who have passed away. Thus, all my older brothers had named their first-born sons with the name of our father, killed when we were children. My son is the only one left named after my father as all my nephews were killed in Europe during the war. Because of the difficulty for the Bolivians to pronounce my son's Jewish name, we all ended up calling him Maxi.

When it was time for my daughter Chana to begin formal studies, there was no Jewish educational institution in Bolivia. While we adapted to our new lives, my daughter began to attend the kindergarten of the Piloto School, a program subsidized by the Bolivian government and that survived thanks to foreign donations. Chana was able to study in that institution thanks to the director, Mrs. Nora Pardovalle. Since my daughter spoke only Yiddish, my brother waited for her every day outside the school for hours, just to assure us that Chana would be able to return safely to the house. My daughter studied up to sixth grade at the Ingavi school and finished elementary school there. Fortunately, the Bolivian Israelite School was opened by that time, where she attended high school and graduated with basic knowledge of the Hebrew language and of Jewish customs and traditions, supporting everything we, as a family, passed down to her.

The Jewish community in Bolivia eventually amounted to 20,000 people in the 1950s. However, many of these families never stayed long enough to take root at all in the country. It was common for them to emigrate to other countries such as Argentina, Brazil, the United States, and Israel. Some of the most powerful reasons that prevented long term establishment were the altitude and climate of La Paz. Because of this, the number of Jews left in the 60s and 70s was much lower, at around 3,500, but we remained united and we found the necessary conditions to preserve the identity and fulfill our customs and traditions.

There were four synagogues in La Paz. I attended the German synagogue because I considered it to be more orderly than the others. I cannot say that I have been very strict with the fulfillment of *mitzvot*. My wife lit candles to mark the beginning of Shabbat, but other than that we did not keep any other customs. My faith had been seriously wounded by the war. This ambiguity in my soul has always accompanied me. On the one hand, there are unanswered questions:

How did you G-d allow all this horror to happen?
Were not many of those who died faithful to you?
Were my mother, my father, my brothers, and my sisters
not good, faithful, religious people?

On the other hand, I feel the certainty inside me that my brother and I could never have survived without the help of some higher power. When we could clearly see the glares of those German soldiers in that barn, who looked at us without seeing us, it was as though G-d placed a veil before their eyes to save us.

My perseverance in the Jewish religion has much to do with the memory of my parents, their love, and their desire that I follow their path through the ancient rituals and traditions of our Rosh Hashana, Yom Kippur, and Pesach holidays, which I always celebrate. After we met Alejandro and Dora Iberklied and their children, we usually rotated, one day at their house and one day at ours. The table was always very big, maybe as a way to honor the memories of our lost loved ones and to never forget them, so that they stay with us and never leave us.

Another man who would always accompany us was Mr. Pearl, a German Jew who was my neighbor in the first shop I owned. For this poor man, the war had left behind some terrible traumas. For example, he had two apartments in different neighborhoods and nobody knew which one he slept in. This was his way of trying to escape the imaginary enemies who would come for him to take him to the extermination camps. We all remember him fondly. He would always bring flowers and gifts for the children.

In the community, there was a good man who worked as a *shochet*[33] Not only was he responsible for the kosher slaughter of hens and cows, but he also functioned as a rabbi at weddings, burials, and other religious rituals. Mr. Chaskel was also an excellent *mohel,* and he was in charge of the circumcision of every Jewish newborn boy. In La Paz, the market was very particular. You could buy anything; the food was fresh and at a fair price. We bought live hens so my children could take them to Mr. Chaskel. He butchered them, but we had to pluck them ourselves. It was a very tedious business and we all had to help.

---

[33] A person certified under Jewish law to slaughter cattle and poultry.

Occasionally, on Sundays, we would all go with Mr. Chaskel to an estate close by, and he would butcher a cow and divide its meat between four families. The advantage was that the meat could be preserved for a long time without needing refrigeration, thanks to the unique climate of the Bolivian capital.

At the time Jewish products were not easy to get. For the Passover holiday, only *matzah*[34] and matzah flour could be acquired. This was spiced with schmaltz (chicken fat) and tasted delicious.

After so many hardships that my brother and I had, who would have thought that we would ever have a table where there would be food left over? Anyone who has ever been as hungry we were during the war adopts an unbreakable rule: food is sacred, you should never throw it out, especially if it is bread.

At times, my neighbor Leiser Klein and I were in charge of making Pesach wine. We ground the grapes and let them marinate in sugar for a couple of months to ferment. This way we had a wine of guaranteed quality.

When we left the neighborhood of Miraflores, we moved into an apartment in a neighborhood in the center of La Paz, on Yungas Street. It was then that Marina Miranda came to work with us. She was still very young when she came to our house from a small town called Moco Moco, near Lake Titicaca. Marina became another member of our family. She became close to us and us to her. She pampered us endlessly and we all respected and loved her. Like my children, Marina learned to speak Yiddish, which became the official language of our house.

Two blocks from our apartment on Yungas street, a Polish Jewish family arrived, coming from Israel, the country they had gone to live in after the war. They settled on Coroico street and we became good friends. Zise Epelbaum and Chipe Feder Epelbaum had three

---

[34] Unleavened Bread. The eating of leavened bread is prohibited during Passover.

children, Lea, Jose, and Abraham. As we had already lived quite a bit of time in Bolivia, we had the good fortune to help them settle down. For a long time, Mrs. Chipe would bring meat and other groceries to our freezer until they could buy one themselves.

Destiny caused the ties that united us with this family to extend beyond time and space. My son Maxi and Abraham Epelbaum have been inseparable since school in Bolivia and their friendship is still as strong as before. Distance has not been able to separate them, and they visit each other often and keep in permanent contact.

On Sagarnaga Street, our dear friends Zelda and Jacobo Iberkleid had a business close to ours. When they arrived in Bolivia, they lived first in Oruro. Like Frieda, they had survived the war in Russia and we shared similar stories. Jacobo would later come to visit us in Costa Rica to see how we were doing. What I never imagined (and this shows the mysterious way in which fate executes its symphony) was that Harry, one of my grandchildren, would marry Shely, the granddaughter of Zise and Chipe, who was also the granddaughter of Zelda and Jacob, as she was the daughter of José Epelbaum and Sarita Iberkleid. This marriage took place in Miami, half a century after we met in Bolivia, and there we shared our experiences with those old friends.

Our financial situation had improved, and we were able to move to a more central area of the capital, in front of the University of San Andres, in a five-story building with ten apartments that was on Villazon Avenue. This change occurred because my wife wanted the school to be close enough for our children to walk there. The neighbors were exceptionally good people, and some were survivors of the Holocaust. We got to share a lot with some of those families, for example with Karol and Sala Tuchschneider, our neighbors next door. My children became very close friends of Lucho and Ana, members of Aguilar Estenssoro's family.

On the ground floor of the building, Gitman and Hinde Mirtembaum had a store called Elite. They lived on the third floor,

84

and the nights when we shared tea and told our lives and stories over and over again were endless nights. They were also survivors of the tragedy of our people in Europe. We were among five to ten percent of the Polish Jews who had survived the war, from a pre-Holocaust population of some 3,500,000 Jews who lived in Poland, before the German invasion.

Those years in Bolivia were beautiful. We all lived as if we were a great big family. I have been able to confirm that the bonds that were formed between the Jews of Bolivia are of an unusual strength, even among people of the same blood. The tragedy, the pain, the loss can come to consolidate links thicker than those of blood relatives. They were good times. We made a living, and our children were growing without the limitations that we had in our childhood and in a relatively quiet environment, where nothing was lacking, and nothing was left over.

I had lived through the nightmare in Europe, perhaps one of the darkest episodes of humanity. It was not difficult for any other environment to seem calm and favorable to me after that. However, that shining tranquility, relative to the Holocaust, was tarnished by periods of great political instability in the country. Often, revolutions ended up overthrowing governments. On those occasions, we had to stay in the apartment for several days, since the university that was in front of our house was one of the places where people gathered most for demonstrations.

Because of this we always tried, among the neighbors, to have food reserves for several days. The mandatory lockdowns served to unite us and consolidate our friendship. I remember how extensive card games were organized in which I did not participate, but my wife did. These games could well be among the Guinness World Record, as they sometimes lasted up to two or three days in a row. The rooms were filled with a sauna-like haze because of the density of the smoke from the cigars.

Another Jewish family lived on the second floor of our building, the Winers. In addition to the husband and wife, they had three children and their grandparents. The grandfather, Mr. Jeffke, knowledgeable in the study of the sacred books, graciously took it upon himself to teach my son and Moishe, (the youngest of their children, who is close in age Maxi) the basics of prayer.

In La Paz, the precedent became established that the boys and girls, once they graduated high school, would go to study outside the country mainly to Israel, the United States, and Argentina. That was how my daughter, Chana, once graduated, went to study first in New York and later in New Jersey. It was then that she met Aaron Goldstein, her husband. They got married in Bolivia in 1971. Aaron's uncle, David Globinsky, traveled all the way from Costa Rica to attend the wedding. During his stay, he stayed at the house of my friends Gitman and Hinde Mirtebaum. After the celebration, Mr. David insisted that Marcos, Gitman's son, should meet his good friend's daughter, Golcha. In fact, they met each other in Costa Rica and they immediately got married. My wife Frieda traveled to San Jose, Costa Rica in 1972, to attend the marriage of the son of our friends.

Sometime before Frieda's trip to Costa Rica, a bloody revolution had taken place in Bolivia. This time, more than any other, it caused us great concern and shock, since my son Maxi was put in danger when he was caught outside a building in front of the university, at the very moment when it was taken by the military. Our own building received many bullet holes. This event, among others, prompted me to look for a new destination for my family. My son finished school and the altitude of La Paz was beginning to be an obstacle for my health. A doctor I visited recommended to me to get away from the 3,600 meters of altitude of the Bolivian capital. At 55 years of age, I felt no fear of starting over in a new land. I was strong and I trusted my survival instincts.

Without much planning, we started to prepare for our trip to Costa Rica. The decision to detach ourselves from our home was not easy. In Bolivia, we had a group of neighbors, friends, and brethren with whom we felt like family. Our dear Marina, whom life paid back for her goodness and kindness, stayed in Bolivia. Marina later got married and moved to Washington, where she achieved the American Dream.

Those years of moving were exceedingly difficult. There were many times that we seriously thought and spoke of returning to Bolivia, but the truth was that by that time, our children, already settled in Costa Rica, could not accompany us. The thought of them being far away made us resist the urge to leave, and instead stay in San Jose.

Chapter VIII

Costa Rica

I

Wars are waged, and only the ghostly protagonists remain, those of us who look into our own eyes without recognizing ourselves. Costa Rica is a fire of life, despite the deaths that many bring with their luggage; but many of us, in the beginning, did not understand this serene yet intimidating landscape.

> *In Costa Rica, the afternoons are so full of such beauty*
> *they collapse on their beholder,*
> *synchronized with the moon.*
> *Costa Rica burns*
> *with the gradual red of the malinches[35]*
> *and the varying hues of the savanna oak.*
> *Why are we the same in the broken reflection of this mirror?*
> *Why is there so much silence*
> *if there are so many songs?*

---

[35] Non-native tree with beautiful flowers that change from burning orange to brilliant red.

Why do the voices of the past rise
in the shelters of the jungle and the moon?

If I can bleed even in this paradise of colors and fears, it is because the world denies me protection. Perhaps I carry inside of me so many stories, lives, and deaths, that the spell of sand, whose passage the wind perpetuates, is the barrier between my happiness and my silence. Only the silence remains.

II

C osta Rica is a small country whose surface spans just 51,100 square kilometers. Its population, when I visited it for the first time, was close to 2,000,000 people. The climate is exceptional. The country thrives in eternal spring with plentiful rainfall and an eternally green landscape. These characteristics make Costa Rica an extraordinary refuge of life, where approximately 5% of the biodiversity in the world is found. Its altitude is so varied and its geography is so diverse that one might find two completely distinct habitats within a radius of a few kilometers.

The conditions of this small Central American country were radically distinct from those of Bolivia. The main difference has to do with altitude and temperature. We arrived in San Jose, the capital of Costa Rica and the most important city of the Central Valley. San Jose is 1156 meters above sea level, and its average temperature is 20.3 degrees Celsius. La Paz, on the other hand, was over 3000 meters above sea level with an average temperature that is much lower than that of San Jose. It is not difficult to understand that this change would be very favorable for our health; especially Frieda's, Yankel's, and mine. In Costa Rica, we could start up a business similar to the one we had established in Bolivia. In this country there was also a small Jewish community, almost all of Polish origin, which allowed me to communicate in Yiddish and in the Spanish I had learned.

The first time I arrived in Costa Rica was with my friend Gitman. Costa Rica was actually not the destination of that trip, but the United States. Afterward, in 1972, my wife traveled to Costa Rica to accompany our friends Gitman and Hinde Mirtebaum to their son's wedding. Even though our stays were very brief, Frieda and I both had a particularly good impression of the country. At Frieda's return from there, the decision was made:

"We will leave Bolivia. We will live in Costa Rica." [36]

That unexpected and sudden news surprised my family. It was logical that it should be so. But everything had developed in my mind and in my heart, which once again showed me the way. The conditions in Bolivia made the change urgent. Maxi had not finished school, so he did not travel with us. My son stayed with my brother Yankel, who had to sell some merchandise and settle the sales of our business. My wife and I arrived in Costa Rica in 1973 and did our best to accommodate ourselves in the new country. It was not easy without our son and my brother. The year felt like an eternity, but finally, the rest of the family who still remained in Bolivia joined us in San Jose. My daughter Chana was living in Colombia at the time with her husband and children.

Arriving in Costa Rica meant starting over; I was 56, Frieda 45, and Yankel 66. It was not easy at that age, but we were always strong and tough people. All the difficulties that we experienced during the war destroyed us, tore off pieces of our soul, mutilated our spirit, and poisoned our dreams forever; but they made us stronger than anyone who had the happiness of not having lived through what we did. I once heard a saying, "Whatever doesn't kill you makes you stronger."

---

[36] Frieda and Abraham became citizens of Costa Rica in 2001.

In Bolivia, we had climbed the class ladder to settle in the middle class, with greater purchasing power and with all our basic needs covered. People like us, who have lived through a war and suffered such hardships, despise the vanity of superfluous luxuries. For me, the priorities have always been clear. Food and other necessities were never lacking in our home. My children studied and prepared adequately for life. In La Paz, we lived in different areas of the city and we always moved to safer and more exclusive places. The climate there allowed us to keep food for a long time, so we bought everything in abundance: sacks of rice, flour, sugar, large cans of oil. Also, the levels of social stratification marked a clear difference between both countries. In Bolivia, there was much less social mobility between the classes.

In the Pitahaya neighborhood, in the center of San José, we found an apartment hotel. We rented a small apartment in which we had neither television nor telephone. There was only one community phone that was available a few hours a day, for everyone who lived in the building. We were tenants in this apartment hotel for two years; then we moved to Paseo Colon, 200 meters north of Pizza Hut. For the move, we borrowed a supermarket cart from Más x Menos. That was how we moved, making several trips and taking our belongings in the little shopping cart.

I must mention and thank the fact that always, in the places where we arrived, we found good people who gave us their friendship and unconditional help. In Bolivia, we made many friends, and when we arrived in Costa Rica, our landlady, Mrs. María Luisa Gutiérrez Israel and her sister-in-law Rose Mary behaved like angels. They were extremely kind and obliging; we never had a reproach from them at all. A clear example of their kindness and solidarity with us is when they decided to transform the rooms into offices. Little by little the tenants were leaving the place until only we were left, but they never pressured us. They respected us until the last day. Only when we found another site and moved did they start the renovations.

It was this that impacted us most: the human factor. The Ticos are friendly, talkative, with a sense of equality vastly different from any in other Latin American countries. Perhaps Costa Rica has taken a more democratic, less conflictive, and violent path. The great social differences that we saw in Bolivia were not so marked in Costa Rica. Its government and its institutions relied heavily on a strong educated, university, and professional middle class. If I asked for an address, it was very frequent the person would accompany me to the site. This for us was unheard of. My son Maxi had an experience that in a few countries of the world could have happened to him. Just arrived, one night with a group of friends he sat in a cafeteria in downtown San José. Suddenly a man got out of a large car and sat at a table next to his. Maxi, at that time he was 18, told me that his legs started to shake when his friends revealed the identity of that man: he was Mr. Pepe Figueres Ferrer, President of the Republic, and hero of the 1948 revolution. Where were the president's bodyguards? Where were the security measures? This anecdote could be enough to understand the democratic idiosyncrasy of this beautiful and particular country. Unfortunately, as in all the world, societies have changed, not always for good.

As soon as I settled in San José, I started looking for work options. Always, from a very young age, I have dedicated myself to trading, and we looked for the possibility of buying a business to provide for my family. I left every day very early. Returning in the afternoon to my house, I had several options to reflect on. All these businesses were located in downtown San José. There came a time when I was about to purchase a small space in the Central Market, but in the end, it was not possible. Finally, we ended up buying a business called Rafael Angel Arguedas #2. We changed the name and called it Comercial Leo, by the name of our first grandson, Chana's son. It was the first business we had in Costa Rica, a bazaar where we sold everything retail. It was never a prosperous business. The money it provided was enough for us to live, to cover basic needs; I was even able to send my son Maxi to Mexico, to study medicine. However, the profits were not enough to place us in a more comfortable economic situation. We stayed with this business for approximately seven years.

At this time, Maxi, close to finishing his training as a doctor, married Irene Rubinstein. We made a happy wedding and started a long friendship with our in-laws Rogelio and María.

We needed some time to understand that the situation in Costa Rica would not be as easy as we previously thought. San José is a small city, and Costa Rica a poor country with very particular economic circumstances. There was a lot of competition in the city, within a radius of a few kilometers. In Bolivia, particularly in La Paz, people had to buy certain goods, such as coats, gloves, and hats. In a tropical country like Costa Rica, people need very few clothes to face daily life. We tried to compensate for these difficulties by working more hours a day and more days a week. We got up very early and opened at six in the morning. It was my brother Yankel, who woke me up daily banging on the door of my room:

"Abraham, it's late!"
"Leave me alone!"
"No. It's late."

We opened before the rest of the locals did, and that saved our business, since often we sold more in those two or three hours than in the rest of the day combined. When the other shops closed their doors, we stayed open, and we also opened Saturdays and Sundays; Saturdays with normal hours, and Sundays closing at two in the afternoon. If we were closing and a client arrived, we would stay open and attend to him without any problem. These extra efforts helped us compensate for the difficulties, but they were a heavy load for us to bear, as we were already elderly.

At a certain point, we felt that our bodies did not respond to the impulses and efforts of our hearts. We thought that the time had come to retire and we made the decision to sell the business. It was not easy, but we were firm with what we had decided.

We stayed retired for a few months. I thought we could face this new stage of our lives, but it was impossible for me and for my brother. It was not easy for us to get used to the idea of being in the house, staring at each other's faces, facing each other without distractions, with all our ghosts, and without an escape. Those months were terrible for us, but I imagine that they were worse for Frieda, who had to endure the pressure of having two time bombs in the house ready to explode.

It was definitely impossible for us to remain inactive, so we bought a second business, located on 8th Street, on the south side of the Central Market. We also called it Comercial Leo like the previous one. We sold everything, but the specialty was shoes. We offered factory shoes, but the highest demand became the handmade shoes manufactured in Costa Rica.

Many of the shoes that we were sold came glued instead of sewed. It was important to me to give the customers added value by guarantees, to assure them that the product was high quality. If we sold a mediocre product, it would lead to the failure of our business sooner or later. On the contrary, if the client received a good product, he would return and also recommend us. So, I made the decision to sew the shoes that were sent to us glued, to provide higher quality. It was not a negligible effort. Esther, who was a faithful and dear employee of ours and who played a fundamental role in our business, came with me by bus to take shoes to a shoemaker for sewing, in the highest quality manner possible.

This was the best business we had in Costa Rica. We finally started to earn more money and improve our economic situation. Not only did it make a living, but we were able to save to buy our first house and think about retirement.

It is important for me to exalt and value my wife's effort, because every day, during so many years of work in Costa Rica, she brought lunch to me and my brother Yankel. We moved on foot or by bus, with the extra weight of years and fatigue. Fortunately, my daughter Chana was already living in Costa Rica, near our house. She worked in San Pedro and always stayed a little later in the office to take us home from the store. Sometimes she would arrive at six in the afternoon and she had to leave because we were not prepared to close ahead of time and in this my brother Yankel was inflexible.

Every achievement I saw as collective; something we all shared. I could not have done anything without the unconditional help of my brother and my children. When Maxi went to Mexico to study medicine, my daughter Chana settled with her family in Costa Rica. Our children and grandchildren were always close to us, helping us with everything, granting us the happiness of their presence, and the pride of seeing them grow up as excellent people and dignified professionals. When December came, my children took their vacations to help us in the store, not to go to the beach or rest. Esther was also especially important for the business.

But my great partner in my life was Frieda. My wife was the strength, the support. She lived not only with me, but also with Yankel, and went through the whole journey with us, from beginning to end. Not only did she work at home, always looking after our children, but she was also two more arms and a heart in the businesses we had. But daily life, relatively calm and peaceful, was affected by an event that changed our lives forever.

In the year of 1983, Frieda became severely ill with a rare disease that had only been diagnosed in sixteen other people in the world. The doctors detected spots in the lungs. Frieda was spitting blood and feeling very weak. Of course, we were very frightened, and all our attention and concern were focused on Frieda and her illness.

Maxi played a fundamental role as a doctor, and as a responsible and supportive son. It was our son who ran the first tests, contacted a health institute in the United States, sent a biopsy, and got Frieda accepted there. My son took her to the National Institute of Health in the United States, where she received an innovative new treatment that was just being put into practice. The treatment, which would then lead to the cure of this terrible disease, was implemented by Dr. Anthony Fauci, an excellent human being and brilliant doctor who treated my wife as if she were his own blood. She spent a whole year under this treatment and then, for six years, she would return to the United States periodically to receive follow-up treatments. After these six years of treatment, G-d granted us the miracle that our Frieda would heal and move forward, overcoming this test.

From the moment she was diagnosed with the disease, our lives changed forever. She, who had always covered all fronts, who fought with us and for us in the business we had, had to stop working full time and concentrate more on herself and on her own survival.

Tackling business in Costa Rica was not easy for several reasons. We were not the young people we had once been, and therefore we did not have the same strength of youth, but we did have determination and desire. The atmosphere of San José is quite different from that of La Paz, and an event took place that made us reflect on the depletion of our energy and the hostility of the world.

One Friday at noon, two men entered the business armed with machetes and with the intention to rob us. At that time, I was 68 years old and my brother was 78. Without thinking, we faced the assailants. It was my brother who first detected the danger and intentions of those men. One of them carried a package with the machete inside. Yankel quickly anticipated his movement towards the weapon and managed to disarm him. While I struggled with him, my brother wounded him on the head using the machete. I wrestled the other guy on the floor. We would not allow them to take anything.

The attackers fled, but we were left emotionally affected apart from being hit and scratched. I asked my brother not to mention it at home. I did not want to worry my family; it seemed unnecessary to me. What could they do? What was done was done and fortunately, we were healthy and alive.

But Yankel could not resist. Maxi had returned from Mexico as a doctor and was working at the San Juan de Dios hospital. My son saw that Yankel had a bruise and asked him what happened. My brother confessed that he felt terrible and broke down in tears. Worried, Maxi asked him what was wrong, so Yankel told him everything.

When my son heard that the criminal who we had confronted had been wounded in the head with a machete by Yankel, it occurred to him that this man might have arrived at the San Juan de Dios. Maxi arrived at the hospital, reviewed the patients' entrance hours, and tracked down the offender, whom he handed over to the Judicial Investigation Agency (OIJ). Yankel later identified the man who had attacked him.

However, when the trial arrived, my brother denied what he had previously accused, and the man was released.

Although my children did not understand Yankel's motives, they were clear to me and I agreed fully. What would we gain from the man's condemnation? Soon he would be free again anyway and would try to take revenge on us.

I cannot stop thinking that this event must have been a miracle. Just like that time in the farm of our distant Poland, when, before the eyes of the Germans, G-d covered us with an impenetrable mist so that those murderers would not see us, even as we saw ourselves reflected in those cold eyes.

In the year 1990, we took the first vacation of our lives. Leo, my oldest grandson, was in Israel and it occurred to me that this was an excellent opportunity to finally get to know Israel. Frieda and Yankel agreed and so we went. We put a sign on the door of the business that read:

"ON VACATION"

Frieda took the opportunity to visit her sister, in whose house we stayed. We spent fifteen days in Israel and then returned to Costa Rica to resume the routine.

But everything comes to an end. In 1995 we made the decision to sell our last business and retire for good. Our energy had abandoned us, and we did not have what it took to continue.

Sometime later, my daughter Chana convinced me to buy a house. For me, this topic had always been taboo. My father was murdered just when he had managed to raise the money to buy the house of which he dreamed. I could not help but cry when the subject was discussed. I could not help but remember that tragedy, the first of my life and the one that scarred my existence forever. When Maxi bought his house, I also cried, as if that act inevitably involved death and tragedy.

However, the house I bought was a blessing. It is a comfortable house, with a garden, in a nice neighborhood, full of beautiful parks to stroll in. My brother Yankel appreciated those spaces and used to walk every day through the parks and practice Tai-chi with some Chinese gentlemen with whom he made friends. My brother maintained this routine until he was 98 years old.

Chapter IX

The Return

I

Is it really possible to return? To go back to the starting point, to see the faces of loved ones, to return to childhood, and to hope? Can a human race retrace the path, invert the flow of sand, untarnish mirrors?

There is a ghostly space in the gaze;
rooms closed in memory;
trunks sealed under penalty of death.
But sooner or later we have to stop running,
and turn our faces back,
face everything that haunts us in nightmares.

To return. To inspect wounds, to go down into the dark basement, and reveal that we have never gone as far as we always thought. To return. We are condemned to go back to a place that was never really beyond our fear.

Dear Yankel,

I have made the decision to write you this letter, in an attempt to assure myself that in this journey, too, you are with me; even when you preferred to stay in Costa Rica.

Don't think that I do not understand you. It is crazy trying to relive all that, to return to the place where we lost everything. It is like opening scarred wounds with a sharp knife, is it not? But it is not, Yankel. These wounds never healed in my soul. They are as open as they have always been. I have never been able to erase those moments, those horrors, and I always made the decision of not forgetting.

I know that you are different. You have never wanted to talk much about what happened. You never questioned G-d, like I did, or if you did, brother, it was deep in your heart. Maybe the actual crazy thing would be to forget, not to cry, not to reproach G-d, not to go absolutely insane. I love you, and in this adventure too, you are with me, although you might not want it. That is why, eventually, wherever you may be, you will have to read this letter written in our blood.

As always, the trip to Europe is draining. The hours flying and the hours spent waiting to fly are many, especially in such a cold and impersonal space as an airport. Chana, Maxi, and Irene's company has been of great importance to me. I feel safe and supported. I am missing you and Frieda, but without the two of you, at my age, it is possible I would not be able to face what this trip means. This is my second time returning to Poland and the first time you did not want to accompany me either. I give you the reason.

The first time was like entering a nightmare like a nebula, which does not allow light to distinguish shapes of things or faces. At that time, I was not prepared. Sometimes I felt like I was going to go crazy. Remember the bones I brought back from the old extermination camps? I had hoped that at least one of those bones belonged to one of our own. It is not easy to assimilate time; lots of water must pass under the bridge. But the pulse that I feel when approaching our destination makes me sure that time has come. It is time, Yankel, to face the ghosts this time. I'm scared to death, but I must. I know that everything I feel is understood, in their own way, by my traveling companions.

When we finally arrived in Warsaw, millions of mixed feelings gathered in my chest and almost prevented me from breathing. All the stories gained a new materiality. You know well that I have never stopped talking about what happened. My children have heard the same thing so many times that perhaps sometimes they have the sensation of having lived it themselves. That has never been my intention, but rather the urgent need to keep alive everything that was taken from us.

Many times, I think it is guilt that has always tormented me; guilt for having saved myself, for not having died as everyone did. I do not know how you handled it; when you lost even more than I did in that hell. As I told you, my brother, when I arrived in Poland, I relived everything again, but in a different way. The experience involved all the senses, and I could hear the screams again and perceive the bittersweet smell of blood and gunpowder.

Before the trip Maxi read articles that could place him in the context of Judaism in Europe. He learned data that even I did not know. Did you know that the presence of Jews in Poland dates back to the year 1000 of the modern era? From the 1600s, there was a massive migration from Italy, Germany, Spain, and other countries to Poland. It seems that this was due to the rights they were given in Poland: to be able to be citizens and have permission to engage in the activities they wanted. They even gave them great facilities on the subject of taxes. I imagine that those advantages, especially in times of crisis, incited jealousy and hatred towards the Jews. This would explain why Jews could not always live with the comfort that these freedoms offered. Outbreaks of anti-Semitism periodically arose; outbreaks that ended in violence, deaths of our own people, and growing restrictions on the activities to which we dedicated ourselves. But in general terms, in comparison with the lives of Jews in other countries such as Russia and Czechoslovakia, Poland was an acceptable place at the time. No more than that: acceptable.

It is interesting to realize that you can be immersed in a situation without a clear awareness of it. More than that, brother, I am sure that we were totally ignorant of what had happened and the historical context that made it possible. Was the behavior of Polish gentiles in the Holocaust not a mystery to us? Was the death of our father really detached from all that?

The violence was like the sea flooding the earth and erasing everything. We only had time to run and many could not do it.

On the first day in Warsaw, we went to Tykocin. It was interesting to be in this town. Obviously, the Poland we knew continues to exist, but in a discreet, sometimes hidden way. A more modern Poland has grown in its place and has a vastly different image. I could tell you, if there were not so much pain inside me and so many terrible memories, that it is a country of great and particular beauty.

Imagine that in Tykocin the synagogue is intact, and the Jewish quarter could serve to reconstruct something of what was our everyday life back then. We found an old temple turned into a Jewish museum. It is really beautiful and tries to recreate the way of life of the Jews before the war. You can see everyday articles and some of the Jewish liturgy.

"What we were, my brother, is now in museums."

If you think about it, we ourselves are worn pieces of a museum of horror that Europe is just beginning to recognize and that today many have even denied.

The beautiful temple is surrounded by houses, and its architecture leaves no doubt that it was a Jewish settlement. Just like our hometown, the Jewish market was separate from the non-Jewish one. One can imagine, without much effort, that the relations that once existed between Jews and Gentiles here were the same as those we experienced; just like in the film "Fiddler on the Roof." We lived together, although not mixed, never suspecting that such a powerful hatred was lurking in their hearts and that, with the arrival of the Germans, they would find the perfect justification for manifesting themselves and satisfying their hunger for blood with our people.

The second day was much harder. I would have liked for you to be here with me, brother. We traveled to Treblinka and arrived at a forest where they built a few monuments, with a few stones carved with names, to never forget the 900,000 Jews that they efficiently murdered in that short year and a half. One of those stones has the name of our village: Parysow. Will I be able to transmit through this letter what I felt there? I do not believe so, brother. Even though we lived through the same thing, I think some emotions are untransferable.

> *There lie the ashes*
> *of our mother, our brothers, our sister, more family*
> *our nieces and nephews...*
> *your wife and your children.*
> *Only you and I remain as witnesses,*
> *like shadows of the dead*
> *who still live, filled with memories and pain.*
> *Here, more than ever,*
> *I have felt the weight of guilt for having survived.*

Everything became complicated in my soul since that fateful moment in which we were thrown from the train. This psychological imbalance has also affected my children and will possibly affect my grandchildren and those to come.

> *I could feel them, brother.*
> *I could hear their voices whispering, all at the same time,*
> *trying to express the details of their infinite journey*
> *on that train from which they could not escape,*

from which they were not thrown.
I could see their eyes, all together, watching me while they asked me,
"Why would G-d...?"

And then I could not hear anymore, because all the voices at once, like a psalmody singing, were like the buzzing of a giant insect that presages death. Then I thought I understood, Yankel. It was only momentary, but then I thought I understood why they threw us off that train. Then I started screaming. I could not contain myself, brother. If you had been here maybe you would also have yelled with me or maybe you would have tried to stop me. But I yelled and I cried out to our mother, and I introduced her to our family, and I spoke to her about my children, and my grandchildren. I told her:

"Here they are, mother. They are alive. Our family name
and our blood live in them."

Then I did not know, Yankel. It was like dying and coming back to life. Treblinka is now a beautiful forest that shows us how indifferent nature is to the tragedy of human beings. One time I heard the idea that humanity could be erased completely from the face of the earth in just one night, but it would not stop the dawn from being so beautiful, even though the human race would not exist to enjoy it.

Maxi, who for a long time we have called Max, was in charge of taking photos during the trip. He was excited about the photos until we reached a pit where many victims' charred bodies are exhibited. The burned bodies do not suffer decomposition. Maxi was not able to take pictures of that horror. On this site, I prayed the *Kaddish*. There could not be a more fitting place on earth to do it, considering the closeness of our loved ones, our family. We were full of pain. I had the impression that the trip helped my children finally fit a face to the story that they had heard since they were little.

We arrived at the hotel drained of energy. We were too agitated to sleep normally. How does one sleep after experiencing pure horror again? Fortunately, Maxi was prepared and he prescribed us all sleeping pills, at least enough to be able to face the rest of the trip.

But in the first hotel we stayed at, in Warsaw, I had an accident. I could not sleep. There were many ghosts that haunted me, many violent images that rushed through my mind, cornering me in the room of that cold and indifferent hotel. I was so agitated that I fell off the bed and hurt my head. Chana, who shared a room with me, was very shocked, as were Maxi and Irene. Initially, they thought that I should have stitches, but the healing they did was enough for me. You can imagine that my children and daughter-in-law were quite worried and, after that night, Chana barely slept; she just sat in a chair by my side to ensure my sleep.

Our next destination was Parysow. I felt like my heart was about to leave my chest. We arrived at Garwolin and it took us three hours to find the cemetery where they buried our father Mortje. I thought that I would recognize the place, but the path has changed much after so many years. I was sure that there was a distance of two and a half kilometers from the center of Garwolin to Lublin.

We took the main route, following those directions, and we arrived at a forested place I did not recognize. Our guide thought we should return to our starting point and then deviate towards an alternative stone path that ran in a similar direction. Repeating the signs that I had in my memory, but we arrived at a forested area very similar to the previous one and I was not able to recognize it either. On the way, we met some young Poles who, when asked, told us that their parents and grandparents told them about an old Polish cemetery located in another place. We went where the boys told us, but it turned out to be another cemetery, not the one we were looking for.

We had lost a little patience when the guide advised us to inquire at the Garwolin Municipality. Upon arrival, we met a derogatory bureaucrat who took little interest in our request for help. My children insisted, and finally, we arrived at the office of the main official, a well-dressed man with modal purposes. When we explained our situation, he put on his coat and did us the favor of taking us to the ruins of the Jewish cemetery, which were hidden among the undergrowth of the forest.

It was the same direction where I remembered it, the same place we went to so many times with my mother and brothers and sister to pray for the soul of our father. Now the cemetery is a thicket. We took photos of the tombs in ruins and did a little bit of looking with the hope of finding my father's name on one of the stones, but it was difficult to read the names and we could not find the precise spot. But we were satisfied, and I recited *Kaddish* for our father.

I would not be capable of explaining to you the energy that we felt in that abandoned place, forgotten by all the inhabitants of Garwolin. So, I partially understood the reason why G-d let us live: we must remember, we must tell the story, bear witness to its truth. What would be left of our past without the memories that have accompanied us? Who would have recited *Kaddish* for those who have disappeared? We are alive, Yankel, and this means that they did not die in vain, or really at all.

I know that none of those present, including the guide or the main official, will ever forget that holy moment in the remote place in the forest near Garwolin, two and a half kilometers from downtown Garwolin towards Lublin, on the left-hand side.

We left the cemetery and headed to Parysow. You have no idea, brother, of how everything has changed. It was very difficult for me to find the street and the house where we lived. With much emotion, we toured the place. I tried to transmit things that you would have felt immediately, without needing my intermediation. We met an old man who gave me directions to the place that was our home. The house number is still the same, the facade is different. The corner house where our brother Moshiche lived also shows a different facade.

I tell you that one of the granddaughters of Paliski with her husband arrived at the first of the hotels where we were in Warsaw.

They treated us with a lot of love and even invited us to eat at their house in Warsaw. Paliski was her grandfather, but it was her father who accompanied us to visit what had been the property of the man in whom our mother placed so much trust. Remember all the good things they did for us, healing my wounds after being thrown from that cursed train. Upon our arrival, we found the stables, the same ones we hid in to save our lives. There they were, eternal, possibly the great-granddaughters of those cows thanks to which we managed to survive. Do you remember how we used to drink the milk sticking to their udders? Such was our hunger and need. I thanked those cows, Yankel, for you, for me, and for all humanity. The kindness of the animals compared to the murderous hatred of human beings. A neighbor approached us and said she recognized me and remembered how we hid in those stables.

With the help of some locals, we were able to orient ourselves to look for the descendants of Bolek, that Polish gentleman who helped us so much during the most difficult years of the war. You know that without their help we could not possibly have survived. I could recognize the place; there is a row of fifteen peasant houses, but I did not know which one of those houses was Bolek's. Maxi got out of the car and approached a family that was chatting in front of one of the houses. He asked them about the exact location of the old house of Bolek. A lady, approximately 60 years old, asked for our identity, in acceptable English. Upon hearing who we were, she was silent for a moment and when she came out of her astonishment she said:

> "I am Bolek's granddaughter. Here we all know the story
> of Abraham and Yankel. They are a legend in our
> family. As children we played in what were their hiding
> places."

After exchanging hugs and tears, I asked the woman if any of her uncles were there. She told me that two lived in Warsaw and that an aunt still lived there.

The Bolek's granddaughter was kind enough to accompany us to her aunt's house, about 100 meters from where she was. While walking, she told us that she was a teacher in the city and that she was enjoying a day off.

We arrived at the house and when we knocked on the door, an old woman who was about 78 years old came out. I immediately recognized little Yanina. Do you remember her, Yankel? She was the most fearful of her family in that time of uncertainty. I once heard her ask her father to hand us over to the Germans so as not to risk being accused and shot for the crime of protecting Jews. I confess that during all these years I remembered her with rancor, but now she was before me, after so many years, and I realized that she had plenty of reasons to fear and prefer to turn us in.

Then shy little Yanina opened the door and looked at us in shock. To everyone's surprise, she could recognize me and with emotion that led me to tears, she told me:

"Pañe Abraham!"

We merged in a hug. None of those who were there could avoid crying. It was a very emotional moment, brother. When Yanina was able to speak again, she asked me,

"Is pañe Yankel alive?"

She was very happy when I said yes that you were alive and that you were 98 years old. She told me something that shocked everyone:

"Pañe Abraham, I thought I would see death first before you."

We separated with blessings. I had trouble sleeping that night, too. The rest of the trip took us to Warsaw and its terrible ghetto. We saw the monuments for the heroes of Warsaw, Majdanek, Kazimierz,

Auschwitz, Lublin, Lodz, Cracow. These cities, before the war, had important Jewish populations. Today only a handful of us are left.

In Warsaw we attended synagogue. Some 150 people had gathered, and we could see a bar mitzvah. Later we participated in the generous *kiddush*.

On the last day in Cracow, we were in the *Kabbalat Shabbat*[37] with a group of locals and an Israeli orthodox delegation with a *chazan*[38] who had a tenor voice. He helped us feel that, despite all the misfortunes, the nation of Israel lives not in the past, but rather in the present and future.

II

Y ou were the hope when there was none left. My only link with the past, with what was my life, ours, the life that was snatched from us without mercy. You were my company in the most absolute moments of solitude, the only light in the pitch blackness. My eternal companion, my infallible friend, my brother. When we had lost everything, my life was your life, my destiny your destiny, my family your family.

How empty would my hands have been without yours to hold?
How lonely would the endless nights of tragedy have been,
fleeing, hiding in the stables, grasping at hope?
What would have happened if you had also died, taken by wolves?

---

[37] The part of the Friday evening service which precedes the regular evening prayer and solemnly welcomes the Shabbat

[38] Singing pray leader of the synagogue.

My path was never without you, brother. In life and in death
I am never without you.

Wandering through the strange crevices
of the labyrinth of life,
the daily details,
the torments in the night,
I am with you.

You will always be with me, Yankel and together we will walk the
infinite paths of eternity.

My brother Yankel was ten years older than me; my only
brother left of the six of us born before the worst tragedy of humanity
began. Despite the age difference, he was thinner and frailer, totally
dependent on my wife, Frieda. He never worried about his clothes, his
food, his medicines.

These needs were met by his sister-in-law. When my children
and grandchildren traveled, first they would buy a gift for my brother;
the prettiest gift was probably for him. His character was also quite
different from mine. He loved to always be well dressed. On Saturday
mornings he would have breakfast in one outfit and then change into
a more elegant one to go to the synagogue. I, on the other hand, was
never interested in clothes or how I looked. It was Frieda who told me
what to wear. Yankel was shy, fearful, and reserved. He did not have as
much initial force as I, who usually reacted more quickly than him,
and with more initiative and confidence. Then he would follow me,
and nothing could stop him. I can assure you that he even worked
harder than me. He was faithful and entirely reliable; a partner who
was always by my side. In all the places where we lived: in Lodz for two
years, in Germany for four years, in Bolivia for twenty-two years, and
in Costa Rica until his death, Yankel was always my partner at work.

He was a good salesman who, despite his limited Spanish and thick Polish accent, always managed to sell his products.

Yankel accompanied me throughout my life and was so faithful and loving to me. When he wanted to leave me for the first time, when G-d called him so that he would rest at the end of his life, I desperate and in tears, hugged him and begged:

"Do not leave me, brother! What would I do without you?"

And my loyal brother, despite his 101 years of age, of fighting, took pity on my pain and asked G-d for a truce to return to my side for a while longer. That was you, Yankel, my brother, best companion than any other that has existed or will exist.

My kind brother was, before the war, a simple and hard-working man. He was a typical Jewish man devoted to his family and his work. He was a shoe repairer. With this honest work, he earned his living to feed his family.

My brother's wife's name was Chana, but we called her Golde. She was the daughter of a rabbi, which was, for a religious family like ours, a great honor. My mother held her in high esteem, and we all considered her a great and educated woman. He had two children, Sure Peiru and Chaim Mortje. It was with this family that G-d blessed my brother Yankel. Then, G-d took away his two families in a heartbeat and left us alone, orphans, lost in the world. With that luggage, full of pain, we began our journey.

I have always wondered why we managed to get out when so many were left there. Why we were saved when so many others died. I answered myself that it was a matter of location. We were located near that small window in the side of the train, only some 30 centimeters squared. That closeness, the product of mere chance, saved our lives. I know very well, dear brother, that you believed in a more spiritual explanation. You, who lost more than me in the war, and even received less, were always more faithful in G-d, more believing. Your faith remained intact even despite tests that would have broken most. Like Job you remained firm, your simplicity and fragility sustaining my strength and decision.

The train carried away your love, Golde. You would always remember her, saying:

"Zi givein a shaine blondinke."
"She was a beautiful blonde."

And you remembered your children. You always said how they were such beautiful children. You talked a lot about a little coat your daughter, Sure Peiru, had. I have always heard that the most terrible pain a human being can face is the death of a child. The natural thing is for children to bury their parents, and not the other way around. Despite that inexplicable pain, which I ask G-d never to have to feel, you remained standing, brother; love and faith saved you.

When we met ten days later and I realized that we were possibly the only survivors of our family, we made the unspoken decision to focus on life, on continuing to fight and to survive. There was no time to ponder our deaths and losses. We had to focus on defeating the death that persecuted us without being able to rest.

Many doubts and questions were silenced. They gnawed away at my soul and never stopped tormenting me.

How can one understand why all this happened to us?
We made no enemies.
We lived peacefully with our traditions
and we took just the basics to survive.
What did we do that was so terrible to others?
Why were our simple lives threatening,
insulting to the ruthless wolves that pursued us?
Why were we, the harmless,
considered the main enemy to be annihilated?

We could not understand then, and we cannot understand it now, even after so many years. We only know that they took our identities, stole our lives, erased our past, and determined our future. The main victims were not killed in the extermination camps. We were the main victims, the millions who were cursed to survive.

Cursed to die with all the memories,
living in a time without time,
in a land forever distant.
The others were taken to Treblinka and we were left
with the knowledge that no one left that place alive.
The people we loved were burned
and we could only watch from afar,
how their souls, in smoke, ascended to the heavens
to call G-d out for his indifference.

Yankel would never again see his loving wife or his beautiful children. From that moment, he and I were the only ones left. And, in fear of that disgrace, of that nameless pain, G-d gifted us both with a new beginning, a new family. To loyal Yankel, G-d gave his third and last family. The promise was sworn:

"You will not die alone. I give you this new family, and
they will grow and be with you, and you with them,
until the day arrives that you shall come and be reunited
with those that came before."

Then we were two, forever. Prisoners of the wolves, we had to escape so that G-d's promise could be fulfilled. We were, from then on, inseparable, and this was our very strength, the secret to our survival, growth, and adaptation to every place and circumstance. We were able to work together out of love and survival instinct. It was part of your personality to let me decide and formulate most of our plans to manage to survive. But what would have become of me without a

115

fellow soldier so faithful and committed? We made a silent, unspoken pact. No one wrote it, we never told it to anyone, and nobody signed it:

"We will never split up."

We died and lived everything together. When the war was over and we arrived in Lodz, only us and the ragged clothes on our backs, we tried to find ourselves sustenance. There I met Frieda. When we got married, even I did not know what would happen with Yankel. I considered that, at least at first, it would be best for my brother to live with us for a while. What began as a request for my wife to tolerate my brother for a while lengthened slowly and progressively. Frieda was just 19 and I know that it was not easy for her to get used to the presence of another man in the house. At the beginning, Frieda asked me:

"How long will your brother be in the house?"

And I would convince her to wait a while longer. She waited sixty-five years.

My brother never argued with G-d; he always maintained spirituality, facing every obstacle with patience. He made the decision to put his life in the hands of this Superior Being who would bring him on the best path. One of those paths was that of celibacy. In honor of his wife and children, he swore to never marry again.

Yankel had exceptionally beautiful features. He was a man of medium height, with an elegant demeanor. His clear blue eyes shone brightly from his face. Many women wanted to meet him, to go out with him, but my brother remained firm, never wanting anyone to replace Golde, of whom he spoke with great love until the end of his days. My brother decided to continue his life without almost ever talking about what happened. He did not regret his losses. He simply lived the best life he could live.

Despite the strangeness of the situation, Frieda always welcomed Yankel with pleasure. She served his food and made sure his clothes were always clean and well-ironed. This portrays my wife as a whole. Even without full clarity, she was sensitive enough to understand that Yankel was my last link with my past, with what I had been. Frieda's goodness was stronger than any doubt and she was with me when Yankel, exhausted of life, finally answered G-d's call, which this time did not give him a new truce.

When my children were born, Yankel was a second father to them. Because of his views on life, he had more enthusiasm to participate in certain activities that required the peace and joy that I had lost. Everything has always been difficult for me. The war left me with no desire to participate in activities that people commonly do. I was not interested in anything other than my family and a bit of conversation that, in my case, always revolved around the tragedy that we lived through in times of war.

So, my brother took my children to the social activities that were unbearable for me; for example, going to the zoo, birthdays, or parties. It was Yankel who told children's stories at night. When my daughter Chana attended kindergarten, she cried because she did not want to stay. It was Yankel who waited for her for hours. Even today in the family we remember his tale of *The Dancing Puppy*, which we continue to tell our grandchildren and great-grandchildren. My children were happy with Yankel. He liked to take them from time to time to eat in a soda shop or restaurant. I did not share this hobby. For me, the ideal is to eat at home. Seeing my table full of food is the greatest of pleasures.

Undoubtedly, my children's relationship with Yankel went beyond that of an uncle with his nephews. They loved him like a second father, and he loved them like his children. Life took away two children in the war and then life rewarded him with two new children we shared. With the passage of time, our grandchildren began to be born and, as the family grew, nobody doubted that our family was also

Yankel's. My grandson Harry, son of my daughter Chana, could not pronounce my brother's name when he was young, so he called him Yukale. From that moment on, the whole family called him Yukale ... Yukale's family.

I was blessed with six grandchildren. They were raised knowing that they had two Gutreiman grandparents, and Yukale's kind character made him the favorite grandfather. After so much pain and tragedy, G-d rewarded my brother with children, grandchildren, and great-grandchildren.

Yukale loved going on vacation with Maxi's family. Irene, my son's wife, and our three grandchildren loved him and spoiled him. That is how we encountered the beautiful beaches of Costa Rica and traveled by land to Nicaragua.

Even over 80 years of age, he enjoyed every minute, just like a child, full of innocence and kindness. Really, my beloved brother was incredible; always happy with everything and always positive. He rarely ever complained. He could sit watching television and any program would fascinate him. Today, people have 80 channels to choose from and none they enjoy; I remember that Yukale needed only one channel to enjoy.

My beloved brother, now that you are not with us, my family, which was always yours as well, remembers you. Rather than crying, we recall your presence and your kindness with joy.

There is a point, Yukale, which turns out to be all points;
a space that is all spaces.
There is always a blurred landscape disfiguring before my eyes,
a light melting into all other lights,
the cold of that morning,
the firelight which warmed me like a coat,
the last light in your eyes, my brother,
my loyal companion of this journey.

All the faces, Yukale, stopped at that moment, even my own face, deteriorating towards nothingness.

A window to infinity,
an insufficient gap to flee from death
for the chance to live the life I have lived,
to inhabit all those uncertain spaces, brother,
without ever being able to detach myself from that moment.

Chapter X

Farewell to This World

My brother Yukale was called, in the end, to the place from which there is no return. This time my pleas and my pain did not matter. This time G-d did not extend his life further. It was extremely hard for me to accept that my brother would no longer be with us, after being my support, my partner, my inseparable companion for so long.

Yukale died at age 101. The knowledge that he was surrounded by his loving, caring family soothed the pain of his absence. Even in these situations, I make an effort to move forward. But I felt that the last link to my family in Parysow was finally ripped out.

My health has slowly deteriorated. 15 years ago, a pacemaker was given to me. Additionally, the appearance of diabetes has limited my diet. However, I must be honest in confessing that I did not surrender myself entirely to these prohibitions. Five years ago, I began to suffer from shortness of breath. This, of course, began to affect my ability to walk long distances, bit by bit. When I visited Poland, three years ago, I had to be taken long distances in a wheelchair.

Although my physical health has been greatly diminished, my family can attest that I keep my mental abilities intact. I have learned to enjoy my routine. In the mornings I love reading the newspaper and then being able to comment on national and international news. My beloved Frieda has never left my side. There are very few things that I enjoy more in life than my daily walks with my wife and daughter.

I have also maintained my hobby of entering massive supermarkets and gazing at all the options of food that I have the ability to buy and enjoy. On Saturdays, I have not stopped going to the synagogue with my son. Sometimes, during my prayers, I would ask Rabbi Miletski:

"Where was G-d during those terrible years in Europe?
Where?"

And the good rabbi, who has supported me so kindly in these past years, would respond:

"Abraham. We do not have the answer to everything."

My life was divided into two parts: before the train, and after. Why couldn't I stay on that train? Every time my family introduces me to someone, I ask:

"Did you tell them how I jumped off the train?"

On Sundays, I go out with my son and daughter-in-law. These outings fill me with the energy to start a new week.

However, time continues to take its toll on my health. My feet have filled with water and each time I respond less to treatment. In recent weeks, it has been difficult for me to leave the house. This final stage of my life is becoming heavier and heavier. In these last few weeks, I spend more time lying or sitting down. Despite the fact that I cannot leave the house, I still enjoy seeing its beautiful garden and the almost constant presence of the variety of birds that surround my feet, accustomed to receiving food.

These last few days I have felt unbelievably bad. I must use oxygen for 24 hours a day. My family comes to visit me every day, staying for several hours. They cannot take me to my room, as it is on the second floor, so I now have a new bed on the ground floor. I tell my son Max:

"I think I have about three days to live."

My dear son, silent with sorrow, does not answer me.

I find myself lying down in my hospital bed and I make an effort to remember my loved ones. I begin: my daughter Chany (Chana Jidis), named after my mother; My son Max (Mortje Izrok), is named after my father. I begin to recall the names that I gave my grandchildren and great-grandchildren and I realize that everyone in my family who is no longer with us has a corresponding descendant of mine that bears his or her name. Am I missing one? No, I'm not missing any. I think G-d, after all, has been very good to me. I do not lose the opportunity, in these last days, to share with my loved ones my deep thanks to G-d for the life he has given me.

Today is Friday night, I am exhausted, and it is difficult for me to breathe. However, I am sitting in the wheelchair at the head of the table with the Shabbat candles, which Frieda has always lit. I have no appetite, but I see my family by my side: my children, grandchildren, and great-grandchildren. They serve me whiskey and I make an effort to lift my glass and tell everyone:

"Lechaim. Lechaim"[39]

---

[39] Yiddish: To Life.

Epilogue

Our father Abraham died on a Saturday morning. After his burial, on Sunday, the shiva began. We faithfully attended our father's Kaddish, which lasted eleven months.

Our beloved Abraham and Yankel were together again. Their separation did not even last long. In any case, we know that G-d's time is very different from ours. We firmly believe that the two brothers met with each other, their grandparents, parents, siblings, and Yankel with his wife and children. On an old train platform they embraced, and they understood that they were last together only yesterday and that now they would resume their love forever. The graves of Abraham and Yankel are together in the cemetery. They are the only ones in this family who are buried in a known place and had their Kaddish. G-d did not allow their names to be erased from the book of life.

On October 26th, 2020,
in the middle of the largest pandemic of the last 100 years,
a great-grandson of our father was born in Jerusalem, Israel.
The baby has the same name as our father
- his name is Abraham Gutreiman.

— Chana and Max Gutreiman

About the Authors

Max Gutreiman Goldberg was born in La Paz, Bolivia in 1955. He currently lives in San José, Costa Rica where he practices as a Medical Internist.

Chana Gutreiman Goldberg was born in Munich, Germany in 1949. She is a sociologist, who previously worked for the United Nations High Commissioner for Refugees. She currently lives in San José, Costa Rica.

Mauricio Vargas Ortega was born in Santa Ana, Costa Rica in 1971. He is a writer, researcher, and professor. As one of the authors of this book, his task was to give a literary structure to the faithful transcriptions of the life stories of Abraham Gutreiman.